*No Trace of the Gardener*

# No Trace of the Gardener

*Poems of Yang Mu*

*Translated by* Lawrence R. Smith and Michelle Yeh

*Yale University Press*    New Haven and London

Designed by Sonia L. Scanlon
Set in Garamond type by Tseng Information
Systems, Inc. Durham, North Carolina.
Printed in the United States of America by
Vail-Ballou Press, Binghamton, New York.

Library of Congress Cataloging-in-
Publication Data
Yang, Mu, 1940–
[Poems. English. Selections]
No trace of the gardener : poems of
Yang Mu / translated by Lawrence R.
Smith and Michelle Yeh.
p.   cm.
Includes bibliographical references and
index.
ISBN 0-300-07070-5 (alk. paper)
1. Yang, Mu, 1940–   . —Translations
into English.   I. Smith, Lawrence R.,
1945–   .   II. Yeh, Michelle Mi-Hsi.
III. Title.
PL2924.S47S55   1997
895.1′152—dc21      97-15641
                        CIP

A catalogue record for this book is available
from the British Library.
The paper in this book meets the guidelines
for permanence and durability of the
Committee on Production Guidelines for
Book Longevity of the Council on Library
Resources.

10   9   8   7   6   5   4   3   2   1

# Contents

# Acknowledgments

*Like many books,* especially collaborative ones, this project has had its share of successes and setbacks, exhilarations and frustrations. We would like to express our deep appreciation for the financial support of the Taiwan Council for Cultural Planning and Development and the Li-ching Cultural and Educational Foundation in Taiwan, without which the book would not have been possible. We would also like to thank Yang Mu, who has provided encouragement and helpful suggestions. Our belief in his poetry brought us together in the first place and has sustained us on our journey from its Chinese starting point to its English destination.

# Introduction

## Michelle Yeh

> *If poetry, or the organic life of culture as a whole, is to*
> *be worthy of persistence, we must seek its definition in the*
> *process of experimentation and breakthrough.*
> Yang Mu, Afterword to *Someone* (1986)

*By 1940,* the year Yang Mu was born under the name Wang Ching-hsien, modern Chinese poetry had traveled a short but treacherous path. In rising against the monolithic tradition of classical poetry, modern Chinese poets were proclaiming a revolution. Led by young intellectuals, many of whom were educated in the West, this revolution intended to liberate poetry from rigid conventions of form, prosody, language, and themes. This literary experimentation was part of China's May Fourth Movement, a wholesale cultural reform and drive toward modernization in the 1910s and 1920s. Modern Chinese poetry was in its infancy during this tumultuous time in Chinese history, when the newly founded republic was on the brink of political, social, and economic chaos. After an avid yet brief exploration of foreign literature—particularly of Anglo-European Romanticism and Symbolism—and applications of these styles to Chinese, poets and other artists turned their attention to national survival. As a full-fledged Japanese invasion became imminent, many poets relinquished their personal visions for a collective one. After China went to war with Japan in 1937 these poets deemphasized their creative freedom and embraced a poetic of social responsibility. Increasing Communist influence in the 1930s and 1940s solidified this change into a creed culminating in Mao Tse-tung's "Talks at the Yen-an Forum on Literature and Art" in 1942.

But poets did not stop experimenting; their work thrived in such vastly different and unlikely places as Japanese-occupied Shanghai, the largest and most cosmopolitan city in China, and the remote south-western mountain town of K'un-ming in Yun-nan Province, which sheltered refugees from the north, including some of the most accomplished poets in the country. The cosmopolitan access to Western trends and the somewhat tolerant cultural policy under Japanese rule ironically allowed writers in Shanghai to do as they pleased while some original Modernist work was being written in K'un-ming by a group of poets affiliated, as professors or students, with Southwest United University, the temporary wartime conglomerate of three of the most prestigious universities in China: Peking, Yen-ching, and Ch'ing-hua. If, by disposition or by chance of access, Romanticism had been most influential among the pioneers of modern Chinese poetry in the 1910s and 1920s, now Symbolism and High Modernism received serious attention among the poets, who were also introduced, in the 1930s, to Futurism, Dadaism, and Surrealism. Some works from this period waited more than thirty years for recognition in the People's Republic of China. The Communist regime, founded in in 1949, ended all free literary expression, and the situation did not change significantly until the late 1970s. Thus, for the three decades after 1949, avant-garde Chinese poetry was almost exclusively found outside mainland China, in particular in Taiwan.

Yet the modern history of Taiwan is no less traumatic than that of China. Exploited first by the Portuguese in the sixteenth century, then colonized by the Dutch and the Spanish, respectively, in the seventeenth, Taiwan was annexed as a province of the Ch'ing (Manchu) Dynasty (1644–1911) in the eighteenth century. When the declining empire was defeated in the Sino-Japanese War in 1895, Taiwan was ceded to Japan, which ruled the island for half a century. This colonial past is a recurrent theme in Yang Mu's poetry. Inseparable from the poet's treatment of the subject is his uncompromised insistence on the dignity and pride of the island, which has demonstrated cultural wealth and spiritual inviolability despite its history of colonialism.

Among his poems is "Zeelandia," written in early 1975. The title refers to An-p'ing, a fortress in T'ai-nan, in southern Taiwan, where the Dutch landed more than three centuries ago. In the mid-seventeenth century the Dutch were driven away by the fleet of Cheng Ch'eng-kung, better known in the West as Koxinga, the Chinese general who intended to restore the Ming Dynasty after it was overthrown by the Manchus. The poem juxtaposes a panoramic view and a closeup of an imminent clash between the Chinese and the Dutch, concatenating "history's broken pages" of rusted cannons and the immediacy of "enemy ships" and "stampeding gunsmoke." The enemy ships refer to Cheng's fleet, and the "I" in the poem is a Dutch officer vainly setting up defense on the rampart. But the poem is far from an angry condemnation of imperialism and a paean to the Chinese victor. The relationship between the colonizer and the colonized is more complex than one between the oppressor and the oppressed. Taiwan, referred to as Isla Formosa (Beautiful Island) in the poem, is compared to a woman ravished by the male colonizer, but the woman exhibits strength and depth beyond the man's understanding and control. While the colonizer is enchanted by the woman's "crisp" accent and slender limbs, he is surprised to find her "cruel mint-scented" breasts "asserting a birthmark." If he relaxes on the broadleaf bed swaying in the subtropical breeze he finds himself losing composure in the cicada drone in muggy summer. His dehumanization and objectification of the woman (she is compared to a "water beast," her cry a "dried-up well" producing "empty echoes") underline his arrogance. However, he admits, "I don't know how to calmly ravish / her new blue flowered dress." The tension between the verb *ravish,* which denotes a violent act, and the adverb *calmly,* which drastically modifies that act, suggests the erosion of the colonizer's smug confidence. The pearls on her "slanting pendants" possibly refer to the Chinese warships about to attack, and the colonizer senses his looming demise: "In my embrace of sulfur smoke, Holland's body / rolls like a windmill." Erotic energy is inextricable from fate, tenderness from violence, lovemaking from war. By the end of the poem, the roles of colonizer and colonized are reversed: "I've come from far away to colonize you / but I have surrendered."

When Yang Mu was born, Taiwan had been ruled by Japan for

forty-five years. Under the policy of the colonial government, he first learned to speak Japanese, the official language at that time; he learned Taiwanese at home. He even picked up some aboriginal languages from the tribes living near his hometown Hua-lien, a beautiful medium-sized town nestled against a mountain range and facing the Pacific Ocean on the east. The multifarious linguistic and cultural background from which he came would grow even richer: he learned Mandarin as a youngster, English as an undergraduate student at Tung-hai University in central Taiwan, and Old English, ancient Greek, Latin, and German as a graduate student at the University of Iowa and the University of California, Berkeley.

Taiwan was retroceded to China at the end of World War II, but the early postwar years under the Kuomintang, or Nationalist Party, were far from peaceful. Harsh living conditions grew even harsher as a result of corruption and discrimination, which led to widespread disaffection on the island. A clash between the native Taiwanese people and the government broke out on February 28, 1947, followed by a brutal suppression that left a deep wound that took decades to heal. The eagerness with which the people had looked forward to being reunited with the motherland was quickly replaced by a bitter sense of betrayal and disillusionment.

After the Communist victory in the civil war and the Kuomintang's retreat from the mainland to Taiwan in late 1949, the reign of White Terror began. Although carried out on a more limited scale and with less drastic measures than Mao's purges, the repression of free expression was not much different from what occurred in Communist China from the 1950s through the 1970s. Books written by mainland writers—now labeled leftist—were peremptorily banned, thus severing the tie between young writers in Taiwan and their mainland predecessors. These postwar writers were similarly uprooted from the native Taiwanese literary tradition. Under Japanese rule, most Taiwanese writers had written in Japanese. With the retrocession, however, Chinese became the only official written language and Mandarin the only spoken language allowed in Taiwan. Implicit in such a policy is the suppression of the local dialect and the native literary tradition. This entails a double deprivation for the writers: prewar Chinese and Taiwanese literature was excluded from the canon and was unavailable to the general public, and older Taiwanese writers had to reeducate themselves in Mandarin in order to continue to write and publish. While a few made the linguistic transition, many were silenced permanently.

Yang Mu is not only one of the foremost representatives of the first generation of postwar writers in Taiwan, he is also a pioneer of native Taiwanese poets. In 1955, when he was fifteen, he started writing poetry, mainly with the encouragement of his Chinese literature teacher Ch'u Ch'ing, a poet and novelist from the mainland. Soon he began editing, with his senior schoolmate Ch'en Chin-piao, a poetry gazette called *The Seagull,* as well as a literary supplement devoted to modern poetry in the *East Taiwan Daily.* He used many pen names at that time, finally settling on Yeh Shan until 1972, when he adopted the name Yang Mu.

In many ways the name Yeh Shan—*yeh* (leaves), a common Chinese surname, and *shan* (fine jade), a given name usually used for women— aptly signifies the style of Yang Mu's early work from the late 1950s through the mid-1960s. It is a poetry that often has beautiful, serene, and majestic nature as the backdrop: stars and forests, mountains and rivers, birds and butterflies, falling leaves and green moss. Against this backdrop a melancholy youth wanders alone, reflecting on love and life, time and death. Such words as *solitude, loneliness, drifting,* and *dream* appear repeatedly. The poetry reminds us of Romantic lyricism. For example, the last stanza of "When Dusk Fills the Sky" (1960) reads:

> When dusk fills the sky, when it fills the sky
> do past and future meet
> to exchange a glance
> or deliver a moment's heartbeat?

The spectacular but short-lived twilight symbolizes the fleeting present, which, like a heartbeat, is precariously situated at the conjunction of past and future. Eluding the grasp of the poet, the present vanishes the moment it appears, like the love evoked in the poem. In its imagery, use of refrain, and theme of the transience of love and beauty, it echoes the famous "A Chance Encounter," written by Yang Mu's predecessor Hsü Chih-mo (1897–1931), the Romantic par excellence of early modern Chinese poetry:

I am a cloud in the sky,
By chance casting a shadow on the ripples of your heart.
　　No need to be surprised,
　　Even less to rejoice—
The shadow vanishes in a wink.

You and I met on the sea at night;
You had your direction, I had mine.
　　You may remember,
　　Better yet forget—
The light emitted at the moment of encounter.

However, the best of Yang Mu's early poetry goes beyond Romanticism. Through a skillful use of fragmentary syntax, wild juxtapositions, parataxis, and repetition he creates an inward—even psychedelic—vision closer to that of the Symbolists and Surrealists. Ambiguity and dramatic tension characterize such poems as "News" (1958), "Footsteps" (1959), and "Bivouac" (1960), in which opposite states of being are simultaneously evoked to suggest an intertwining of the conscious and the unconscious, of internal and external reality. "The Woman in Black" (1958) is another fine example:

Drifting here and there between my eyelashes
standing outside the door, remembering the ocean tides
the woman in black is a cloud. Before the storm

I wipe the rainy landscape from my window
wipe the shadow off the wutong tree
wipe you off

Ambiguity and tension derive from the verbs ("drifting," "standing," "remembering"), which depict the woman in black as both elusive and concrete, both visionary and physical. In contrast with the first stanza, with its tantalizing indeterminacy, the second stanza is deceptively simple, with its one and only verb, "wipe." The repeated word emphasizes the speaker's will to erase the image of the woman from his mind. But just as it is futile to wipe a dark cloud from the window to forestall a storm, his effort to "wipe you off" only reveals his inability to escape her haunting vision. The cloud image further suggests a dangerous attraction. There are other memorable images from Yang Mu's early poetry, including the "howling stars" in "Footsteps" (1959); the horse's "plum-blossom prints" in "Silence" (1962); and the "white flower with the silence of Time in its hand / reaching from stone steps toward the edge of the well" in "Blue Smoke" (1963).

A major motif in Yang Mu's early poetry is time and memory. "On the Cliff" (1963) presents a spring scene full of life and vigor: blooming sunflowers, returning partridge, spring water, and woodcutting. The luxuriant forest of majestic trees reminds the poet of the splendor and strength of a "thousand Roman spears and columns," which further evoke the legend of Romulus and Remus. However, the train of thought ends in homesickness. Rome is no more. In time trees grow, then are cut down to build palaces that are destroyed. The poet is reminded by "you," in the last stanza, that time brings an end to everything, even as trickling water is capable of drilling through the thickest rock over time. Despite all the human activities—camping, hunting, making love—the poet realizes the inevitable advance of time. Unlike the traditional Chinese view that time is cyclical and to be accepted and integrated with the human, the poet sees time as both essential and threatening to human existence. For young Yeh Shan, the most frightening aspect of time is not the change that time brings but its ceaseless progression without human presence or participation. Further, since time is a human creation and an artificial concept to begin with, its independence from human existence takes on a sinister irony. Memory, then, becomes a way of humanizing time; it serves as a testimony to humanity, whereas its absence—oblivion—is in essence no different from death.

For the poet, then, memory is life's triumph over time, as opposed to oblivion, which is the ultimate kind of death. This is the dominant theme of another early poem, "To Time," which begins: "Tell me, what is oblivion / what is total oblivion?" A series of images of decay and death then follows—fallen fruit, decrepit moss, autumn, dust, buried flower scent, and a falling star. Death is equated with stillness, rigidity, and silence suggested by the images of stalactites and stalagmites, the fountain solidified into a "hundred statues of nothingness" and an echoless mountain grove. Finally, the absence of motion and sound is depicted as eternal darkness, in which the light of memory is extinguished.

Intertwined with the theme of memory are love and poetry, all of which are seen as ways of transcending oblivion, the obliteration of memory by time. If these motifs run through Yang Mu's oeuvre, the style with which they are treated changes significantly over time. By 1972 the poet had left behind the youthful lyricism tinged with melancholy and nostalgia. His poetry became sharper and harder. The introspective, somewhat narcissistic speaker in the early work gave way to a more complex, detached, ironic, self-reflexive narrator; the backdrop of nature that dominated before also expanded to include both natural and urban landscapes. The dramatic tension underlying some of the early poems resurfaced in full force. For instance, the use of dramatic monologue in "Chi-tzu of Yen-ling Hangs Up His Sword," "The Second Renunciation," and "Floating Fireflies," all written in 1969, suggests the contour of a complex psychological story: whether it is about a disillusioned Confucian scholar in the first poem, an outlaw cynical about religion in the second, or the ghost of a murderer who mistakenly killed his beloved wife in the last. The contrast between the early and later work of Yang Mu is probably best seen in the way love is treated. The tender lyricism in the early work is replaced by an eroticism that blends longing and ennui, courtship and withdrawal, physical immediacy and contemplative detachment. As he says in "Lovesong" (1972): "amorous longing / has become a bitter song." "Prophecy" begins and ends with the image of the "chaotic and spasmodic pleasure of life." The imagistic progression from explosion to relaxation in the poem suggests the ebb and flow of desire, also expressed in hyperbolic terms in the transition from the glorious T'ang Dynasty to the weakened, chaotic Five Dynasties. The suggestive juxtaposition of the grand and the personal is similarly seen in "Partridge Sky" (1974):

> Spreading out like this is good
> Intermittent musical notes
> eyes are the lanterns
> of the Decadents, body hair the
> prairies where the Crusaders camped

The languid yet gnawing eroticism is best summarized by the recurrent image of a snake. It appeared as early as 1960 in the poem "When Dusk Fills the Sky": "the narrow path you've walked / is a tipsy mottled snake." In the poet's mature period the snake is often associated with sexual desire that is darkly tempting, even beyond control. Hence the yielding to desire in "Lovesong," which begins, "When snakes / like pouring rain / . . . swim to the storm sitting in the dark." The storm is in fact the poet's "tired self." The snake evokes the phallus in the 1973 sonnet sequence "I imagine you in a / garden of floating fireflies / listening to night birds flapping on the erect snake god." In his recent poetry the snake is transformed to take on different meanings, which I discuss later.

Yang Mu's language is a blend of the literary, which is derived from classical Chinese poetry and prose, and modern vernacular. Yang Mu is one of the few poets who succeed in assimilating the classical tradition into modern poetry. Some of his titles, such as "Partridge Sky," "Departing," and "Crows Crying in the Night," come directly from classical poetry. Others, like "Subtle Fragrance" and "Floating Fireflies," are well-known images from classical poetry. He alludes frequently to classical poetry (by Li Po, Tu Fu, Han Yü, Ssu-ma Hsiang-ju, T'ao Yuan-ming, and others) and literature (including *The Water Margin* and *Dream of the Red Chamber*). The syntax of Yang Mu's poetry is radically innovative. The sentence is still the basic unit of thought, but the poet turns it into an expansive discursive space in which the shifts and turns of thought are introduced with parenthetical asides or concatenated clauses and phrases. Syntax is inseparable from the semantic and structural aspects of a poem, as "Let the Wind Recite" (1973) demonstrates. The poem is divided into three sections and runs sixty-three lines long. The first forty lines are, strictly speaking, but one subjunctive clause, beginning with "If," which is then repeated four times. These forty lines conjure up the trials and tribulations that the lovers have to endure before they can be united. Corresponding to love's tortuous path is the rotation of the seasons: the poem begins with summer, progresses through autumn, winter, and spring, and returns to summer, with which the poem ends. The circular structure symbolizes not only the passage of time but, more important, the perseverance of the lovers and a sense of completion. The circular structure, in which the poem begins and ends with the same image or motif, is common in Yang Mu's poetry; along with refrains and repetitions of key images or words, it achieves an incremental rhythmic and semantic impact. Although as a rule he does not use rhyme, much attention is given to the form of the poem, which ranges from free verse to the sonnet, and he has probably written more sonnets than any other modern Chinese poet. For him the sonnet remains the most suitable form for love poetry, though he did use the form in the 1980 sequence for his newborn son Ming-ming. He also often uses musical forms; such terms as *etude, nocturne, rondo,* and *ballad* appear in many titles. Compared with other forms of art and music, sound in general—droning cicadas, chirping birds, pouring rain being but a few of the recurrent sounds in the poems—is prominent in his poetry. The imagery in Yang Mu's poetry is complex, fusing the sensuous and the abstract, the naturalistic and the existential or metaphysical. Although essentially a lyric poet, he often projects lyricism into a narrative frame characterized by mystery and tension, and his experiments in the narrative poem also led to the composition in 1976 of a verse drama of more than two thousand lines. It is this relentless experimental spirit that has earned Yang Mu widespread recognition as the foremost avant-gardist in modern Chinese poetry.

Although avant-garde writers and artists in Taiwan in the 1950s to 1970s were viewed by the Kuomintang government as ideologically suspicious and were subjected to censorship and harassment, these experimenters in literature and the arts sometimes escaped downright persecution because of their intrinsic obscurity and ambiguity. The regime had difficulty deciphering their work, so much of it slipped by the censors. But even if it was published it would sometimes be confiscated later on. Under these precarious circumstances Chinese avant-garde poetry thrived in Taiwan after 1949. Because they had little access to Chinese poetry of an earlier period, avant-garde poets turned to foreign poetry, especially that of the Modernist tradition of the West. In 1953, Chi Hsien (b. 1913), who had established himself as a promising poet in Shanghai in the 1930s and 1940s, formed the Modern Poetry Society and published *Modern Poetry Quarterly.* Three years later Chi Hsien founded the Modernist School; in its manifesto he urged his fellow poets to be discriminating advocates of the "spirit and essence of all new poetry schools since Baudelaire . . . including Symbolism, Post-Symbolism, Cubism, Dadaism, Surrealism, Neo-Expressionism, American Imagism."

Yang Mu recalled years later that he had been an avid reader of *Modern Poetry Quarterly.* He corresponded with many poets outside of his hometown—those of the Modernist School and also those from other poetry groups thriving in Taiwan in the 1950s and 1960s. He visited them in Taipei during breaks and spent long nights passionately discussing poetry: Rimbaud, Lorca (whose *Gypsy Ballads* Yang Mu translated into Chinese in 1966), Eliot, Pound, Yeats (whose poetry was recently translated into Chinese by Yang Mu), Breton, Rilke (Yang Mu wrote his own version of *Letters to a Young Poet* under the title *The Completion of a Poem*), Keats, Milton, Dante. The list goes on.

Early on, Yang Mu was also associated with young artists (the Fifth Moon Group and the Orient Group) and fiction writers (for example, Wang Wen-hsing, to whom he dedicated the poem "Almost Number Two: Every Summer," included here, Pai Hsien-yung, and Wang Chen-ho, all of whom now enjoy international reputations). They were simultaneously engaged in the avant-garde in various forms and media. During this fertile period Yang Mu was a leading light in avant-garde poetry, a dynamic force in the golden age of artistic experimentation in Taiwan. He influenced not only Taiwanese poetry since the 1960s but also mainland Chinese poetry when it was finally given some breathing room during Deng Xiaoping's regime in the late 1970s. The revival of poetry in contemporary mainland China is best represented by "Misty Poetry," the name used to describe the work of a loosely identified group of young avant-garde poets who include Bei Dao, Yang Lian, Gu Cheng, and Shu Ting.

From the beginning, modern Chinese poetry looked to foreign — predominantly Western — poetry for inspiration and alternative modes of writing. In Taiwan under Japanese rule (1895–1945) modern Japanese poetry, which was itself indebted to Anglophone and European poetry, was an additional influence on native writers. It is easy to see why modern Chinese poetry is characterized by a cross-cultural configuration of images and ideas. This is especially true of Yang Mu's work. As Stephen Owen of Harvard University points out, "[Yang Mu] is a poet who works with the materials that he has, and those materials include a sense of poetic and cultural history that transcends the cultural division of the 'West' and China. He has become bicultural. . . . [Yang Mu] offers the largest hope for the future [of Chinese poetry] because he draws two disparate histories together" (*The New Republic*, February 22, 1993).

At the most obvious level, Yang Mu's biculturalism can be seen in his wide-ranging imagery, references, and motifs, which straddle China and the West. He draws not only on classical Chinese poetry and prose but also on Western literature and culture. Allusions abound in his work, including references to ancient mythology (Narcissus, Athena), religion ("Theology," the Bible, Crusaders, Easter), history, and, of course, literature (Virgil, Marlowe, Dryden, Wordsworth, Emily Dickinson). The recounting of a mysterious, devastating journey in "Fable No. 2: Yellow Sparrow" (1991) reminds us of Keats' "La Belle Dame sans Merci." "Frost at Midnight" (1985) echoes Coleridge as well as late Yeats. His equal erudition in Chinese and Western classics gives him a perspective from which to reflect on the two cultures. "Chi-tzu of Yen-ling Hangs Up His Sword," for instance, draws on Chinese history to critique the Confucian orthodoxy that, with its rigid, narrowly conceived moral and literary institutions, is but a degenerated form of the original Confucianism. Tradition here is used ironically to expose its deficiency; it is evoked only to be undermined.

"Three Etudes: The Snake" represents a radical reading of the Christian myth of the Garden of Eden. It defends the snake as the angelic emblem of beauty, seeing a parallel between the snake's androgyny and the amoral essence of beauty, which transcends the Christian dichotomy of good and evil. But perhaps most significantly, Yang Mu's poetry powerfully fuses China and the West in the way the poet perceives human experience as in tune with the cosmic rhythm of nature. If this view bespeaks an affinity with Chinese philosophical tradition—a belief in the fundamental correspondence between the human and the natural realm—it champions at the same time the Romantic spirit of quest and transcendence.

Yang Mu's biculturalism is based on first-hand experience with the West and a classic education in the best Western literary tradition. Paul Engle, founder of the Iowa Writers Workshop, came to Taiwan in spring 1963 to scout for new talent. He was referred to Yang Mu, then an English major at Tung-hai University, by the poet Yu Kwang-chung and the fiction writer Wang Wen-hsing. Once in Tai-chung he read the few poems that Yang Mu had translated with the assistance of his English professor. Deeply impressed, he invited Yang Mu to go to Iowa after he graduated and completed his mandatory military service. After some hesitation Yang Mu accepted the invitation, and he left in 1964 for the University of Iowa, from which he received an MFA in 1966. At the encouragement of the late Shih-hsiang Ch'en he then went on to Berkeley, where he received a Ph.D. in comparative literature in 1970.

Yang Mu's decision to remain in the United States after graduation from Berkeley was perhaps more than anything else a protest against Chiang Kai-shek's regime—not only against its repression of free speech and press and its entrenched discrimination against the native Taiwanese but also its compromises of Taiwan's dignity and autonomy in its concessions to such major foreign investors as the United States and Japan. The latter theme underlies "Kao-hsiung, 1973." On a tour to the free-trade zone in Kao-hsiung in southern Taiwan the poet notes sarcastically the discrepancy between the pride with which the senior official who guides the tour obviously speaks of Kao-hsiung as the "largest Chinese harbor" and the shame the poet keenly feels on seeing "all thirty-five thousand female workers leaving work at the same time." The Taiwanese women workers who provide cheap labor to foreign investors symbolize the economic exploitation to which Taiwan was being subjected as a developing country. The English words peppering the official's speech and the poet's repeated references to himself as "sick" reinforce the criticism. It is hardly surprising that the poem did not escape censorship: it was literally ripped out of Yang Mu's book of poetry days after its publication in Taiwan.

Since 1970, Yang Mu has been teaching Chinese and comparative literature at American universities, including the University of Massachusetts at Amherst, Princeton University, and, for the past twenty-two years, the University of Washington, Seattle. During his long sojourn in America he has continued to play an active role in Taiwan's cultural scene, not only through his writings, which have won every major literary prize, but also as a speaker at scholarly conferences, a referee at annual poetry and prose competitions, and a visiting professor at the National Taiwan University in 1975–76 and 1983–84.

Many of Yang Mu's poems deal with his hometown or Taiwan in general, and they reveal the poet's most intimate thoughts and feelings. In "Hua-lien" he speaks with the Pacific Ocean; he looks to it as an older and wiser dragon (Yang Mu was born in the year of the dragon) for guidance and consolation. "Looking Down (Li-wu Stream, 1983)" was written when the poet revisited his hometown, to the north of which the river flows. Standing on a cliff overlooking the river the poet sees himself as a "survivor" of life's turmoil and a wanderer who has returned. He confides in the Li-wu Stream, compared to the lover who both accepts him unconditionally and complains of the long intervals between his visits, both reminding him of irrevocable youthful passion and seducing him with the primordial mystery of love and life "where no one has ever been." "Manuscript in a Bottle" was written earlier on the west coast of Washington. The opening images shuttle between the past, present, and future, creating a temporal layering that parallels the poet's surging homesickness and the succession of roaring waves before him. At the end of the poem, Yang Mu imagines himself walking into the Pacific Ocean:

> if I submerge myself
> seven feet to the west off this lonely shore
> will Hua-lien, my Hua-lien in June
> start a rumor about a tidal wave?

In the sky-high tidal wave blurring the boundary between heaven and earth, home and the land of expatriation, the microcosmic self and macrocosmic nature are merged.

Yang Mu has played many roles simultaneously and successfully. Besides producing scholarly work in both English and Chinese, since 1960 he has published ten books of poetry, a play in verse, seven books of prose, two Chinese translations of poetry, and two collections of essays and editorials. For years he has run the Hung-fan Bookstore, one of the most popular publishing houses in Taiwan. He has edited many collections of Chinese literature—modern and classical, poetry and prose.

These roles are the result of conscious choice, and they reflect Yang Mu's ideal. "When I study literary history, especially when I read the chapters on a major poet, my first response often is: he not only did these but also strove to do those other things. Besides poetry in various forms, he also wrote expository discourse, pamphlets, scholarly treatises, annotations and commentaries, prefaces and travelogues, tomb inscriptions and epitaphs, drama and fiction, etc., etc. This is so enviable, so worthy of emulation. What an upright, refined, brilliant, multifaceted life of culture this is." The same admiration also rightly belongs to Yang Mu, whose work has been pivotal in the development of modern Chinese literature. As a poet he has achieved canonical status in Chinese-speaking communities all over the world. He holds one of the most important places in Chinese literary history.

# Yang Mu Chronology

1940     born Wang Ching-hsien in Hua-lien, Taiwan

1946–52  matriculated at Ming-yi Elementary School, Hua-lien

1952–58  matriculated at Hua-lien High School; started writing poetry and publishing it in local and Taipai newspapers and journals

1958     failed the university entrance examination; went to study in Taipei, where he befriended many poets, including Chi Hsien, Huang Yung, Lo Fu, Ya Hsien, Ch'u Ko, and Hsiung Hung; became editor of the poetry journal *Epoch*

1959     matriculated in history department, the Christian Tunghai University, Taichung

1960     transferred to the foreign languages and literature department; published first volume of poetry, *By the Water's Edge* (Taipei: Blue Star Poetry Club)

1963     graduated from Tunghai University and did mandatory military service on the frontier island Quemoy; published second volume of poetry, *Flower Season* (Taipei: Blue Star Poetry Club)

1964     attended the Iowa Writers Workshop (directed by Paul Engle), University of Iowa

1966     received MFA from the University of Iowa (thesis title: *The Lotus Superstition and Other Poems*); published third volume of poetry, *Boat Lantern* (Taipei: Wen-hsing Bookstore) and *Collected Essays of Yeh Shan* (Taipei: Wen-hsing Bookstore)

1966     entered the doctoral program in comparative literature at the University of California, Berkeley; published a volume of selected poems, *No Ferry* (Taipei: Cactus Press); published Chinese translation of Federico García Lorca's *Romancero Gitano* (Taipei: Modern Literature Magazine)

1970     received Ph.D. in comparative literature from the University of California, Berkeley (dissertation title: *Shih Ching:*

*Formulaic Language and Mode of Creation*); became assistant professor in Chinese and comparative literature at the University of Massachusetts, Amherst

1971     moved to the University of Washington, Seattle, where he teaches today; published fourth volume of poetry, *Legends* (Taipei: Chih-wen Press)

1972     adopted the pen name Yang Mu

1974     promoted to associate professor, University of Washington, Seattle; published (in English, under the name C. H. Wang) *The Bell and the Drum:* Shih Ching *as Formulaic Poetry in an Oral Tradition* (Berkeley: University of California Press); published a book of literary criticism, *The Traditional and the Modern* (Taipei: Chih-wen Press)

1975     visiting professor in the department of foreign languages and literatures, National Taiwan University, Taipei; published fifth volume of poetry, *Manuscript in a Bottle* (Taipei: Chih-wen Press)

1976     published a volume of lyrical essays, *Tree Rings* (Taipei: Ssu-chi Press)

1977     published a volume of miscellaneous essays, *The Spirit of Berkeley* (Taipei: Hung-fan Bookstore)

1978     published sixth volume of poetry: *Song of the Big Dipper;* also published *Collected Poems of Yang Mu,* vol. 1: *1956–1974* (Taipei: Hung-fan Bookstore)

1979     visiting professor in the department of East Asian studies, Princeton University; published a collection of literary criticism, *Literary Knowledge* (Taipei: Hung-fan Bookstore)

1980     published verse drama *Wu Feng* and two (his seventh and eighth) volumes of poetry, *Forbidden Games* and *Seven Turns of the Coast* (Taipei: Hung-fan Bookstore)

1981     promoted to professor of Chinese and comparative literature, University of Washington, Seattle; edited two volumes of *Anthology of Modern Chinese Prose Essays* (Taipei: Hung-fan Bookstore)

1982  published a volume of lyrical essays, *The Seeker* (Taipei: Hung-fan Bookstore); edited *Feng Tzu-k'ai: Selected Works* (Taipei: Hung-fan Bookstore)

1983  visiting professor in the department of foreign languages and literatures, National Taiwan University, Taipei; edited *Chou Tso-jen: Selected Works* (Taipei: Hung-fan Bookstore)

1984  published a collection of literary criticism essays, *Origins of Literature* (Taipei: Hung-fan Bookstore); edited *Hsü Ti-shan: Selected Stories* (Taipei: Hung-fan Bookstore)

1985  published a collection of editorials written for the *United Daily,* one of the largest newspapers in Taiwan, entitled *Interchange Path* (Taipei: Hung-fan Bookstore); also published *Annotation on Lu Chi's Rhyme-Prose on Literature* (Taipei: Hung-fan Bookstore) and the edited volume *Hsü Ti-shan: Selected Essays* (Taipei: Hung-fan Bookstore)

1986  published ninth volume of poetry, *Someone*

1987  published autobiographical prose *Mountain Winds and Sea Rains* (Taipei: Hung-fan Bookstore) and a collection of miscellaneous essays, *Flying over the Volcano* (Taipei: Hung-fan Bookstore); edited *Hsü Chih-mo: Selected Poems* (Taipei: Hung-fan Bookstore)

1988  published (in English under the name C. H. Wang) *From Ritual to Allegory: Seven Essays in Early Chinese Poetry* (Hong Kong: Chinese University of Hong Kong Press)

1989  published epistolary prose *The Completion of a Poem* (Taipei: Hung-fan Bookstore) and the two-volume *Anthology of Modern Chinese Poetry,* coedited with William Tay (Taipei: Hung-fan Bookstore)

1991  published tenth volume of poetry, *Complete Fable,* and autobiographical prose, *Returning to Zero Coordinates,* a sequel to *Mountain Winds and Sea Rains* (Taipei: Hung-fan Bookstore)

1991–94  professor at the Hong Kong University of Science and Technology

| 1993 | published a collection of essays on aesthetics, *The Skeptic: Notes on Poetical Discrepancies* (Taipei: Hung-fan Bookstore); English translations of poetry published in *Forbidden Games & Video Poems: The Poetry of Yang Mu and Lo Ch'ing,* translated by Joseph R. Allen (Seattle: University of Washington Press); edited and annotated *Anthology of T'ang Poetry* (Taipei: Hung-fan Bookstore) |
| --- | --- |
| 1995 | published a collection of lyrical essays, *Star Map* (Taipei: Hung-fan Bookstore), and *Collected Poems of Yang Mu,* vol. 2: *1974–1985* (Taipei: Hung-fan Bookstore) |
| 1996 | dean of College of Humanities and Social Sciences, National Dong Hwa University, Hua-lien; published a collection of lyrical essays, *A Hawk Perches at Noon* (Taipei: Hung-fan Bookstore) |
| 1997 | edited *Hsü Chih-mo: Selected Prose* (Taipei: Hung-fan Bookstore); published *Selected Poems of W. B. Yeats,* edited and translated into Chinese, with introduction and annotation (Taipei: Hung-fan Bookstore) |

# A Note on the Translations

*According to* common practice in Taiwan, we use the Wade-Giles system of transliterating Chinese names throughout this book, except for those names already well known to English-speaking readers in the Pinyin system.

# Part One
## 1958–1970

# The Woman in Black

Drifting here and there between my eyelashes
standing outside the door, remembering the ocean tides
the woman in black is a cloud. Before the storm

I wipe the rainy landscape from my window
wipe the shadow off the wutong tree
wipe you off

1958

# News

None. At the harbor I measure my paleness
with a compass

On the road home dead birds
with wide open, laughing eyes
A rifleman wipes sweat from his brow in the teahouse
watches the scenery . . .

For the ninth time we talk about the clouds
but the dim-witted girl is always beautiful—
even though the slab's green moss is crushed
and chimneys are reckoned
she still loves to laugh, she's still so beautiful

For the hundred and seventh time we talk about the clouds
Yes, she still loves to laugh, she's still beautiful
there are still dead birds on the road
the rifleman still wipes sweat from his brow in the teahouse
watches the scenery . . .

1958

# Footsteps

Walk with me into cicadas humming, into fretfulness
Count horses on the entablature
dust-kicking chestnut horses
Calculate age by the river's edge
Sleeper, your hands are pythons

He walks, a shifting shadow, slowly rises
through the palace
to where I sit cross-legged
leaving that empty space to me
yesterday's me

The spot where you drew water from the river
I turn to stare
A blue gourd floats
so do the traveler's lips
Give me ashes, loneliness in clamor
A rosary from the future moon and stars
counting the beads, you put out the light I sought

North-northwest, beautiful fire-watcher
coming from the forest, do you hear stars howling in the east?
The moon to the right, we cross the river at high speed

1959

# Bivouac

Drumbeats off to the right
birds in despair
in profound despair

Yesterday's gunshots have not returned
When shall we cross the river
go to the deserted fortress to smoke
doze off, think about yesterday's eyes
or someone's eyes?

With butterflies for my pillow
the lowest star in the south hanging next to my ear
I turn over to poke the fire —
a mountain rises from my forehead

1960

# When Dusk Fills the Sky

When dusk fills the sky
there you stand, the pagoda's shadow retreating from your skirt
Crimson hillside
the narrow path you've walked
is a tipsy mottled snake

Vega and Altair at opposite ends of the sky
you will feel sad for the young man
strolling before the rail
by the edge of your river

When dusk fills the sky, when it fills the sky
do past and future meet
to exchange a glance
or deliver a moment's heartbeat?

1960

# Narcissus

Stars from another time whisper behind us
we quarrel for no particular reason
Settling into a lullaby
I count as they fall into the valley, become fireflies
and flit around our ankles of starlight, flower shadow

This may be a barren place
but we are ferrying in the same boat

Before we know it we've slipped down
time's current, across the seven seas
a thousand years just a dream. In the sky-high waves
I turn to find you gray at the temples

In Greek classics, Narcissus bends to gaze at himself—
here and now the stars whisper behind us
Sitting face to face by the north window
we dreamily exchange old yellowed letters

1961

## The Town Where You Live

The beach there is like a satin ribbon
slenderly, whitely embracing
the town where you live like a smooth mirror—
wind and clouds, the moon and stars glide across it
a hundred acres of soft sunlight gathering

The sun shines for your straw hat alone
The town where you live stretches out
its ancient arm and outside your window paints
an embassy on the riverbank, a college on wavelets napping in the harbor
You walk toward them, you are the sunset

But this is not my town
when stars rise above your shoulders, you are twilight
I take my time tying up the boat
"My home lies behind the mountain
where the beach is like a satin ribbon"

1961

## Passing Through Peach Blossoms

When I pass through peach blossoms, solitude
is a single evening star on a distant peak
Night is beyond my holding! Fallen leaves depart the empty mountain
drifting like colorless clouds
Someone plays flute on the riverbank in lonely twilight—
garden rain like willows in March, you once cried in the wind

No more drifting, no more
When I pass through peach blossoms, against lonely
twilight reflected on a single broken leaf
I will lie under this tree so you can find me
My solitude is the evening star
Hurry, hurry across the river to find me

1962

# Silence

April drifts down from the treetops
from the hillcrest
shrouded in fog
A horse saunters by, leaving plum-blossom prints on the path

In the deep of night
a young man sits on the steps of the Mountain God Temple
April drifts down the hillcrest
tiny yellow flowers from treetops

1962

# Flowing River

No flaming pomegranate in May, spring passes quietly
Setting a ribbon afloat, a hyacinth sits on the slope
Darkness falls around me, mountain wind leaves little behind
but a corner of dusky sky, its lacy clouds, and willow catkins
I lean against a felled tree
whose rustling flows endlessly on

I won't sing any more, my dear
Spring has turned me into a young girl in a red dress
chasing the bright butterfly of a chiming bell
In sadness I lie down, become a new grave
listen to the vibrating bell from the other side of the river
Spring passes, quietly taking me away

1962

# Questions for the Stars

*And . . . on thy breast I sink.*

Robert Browning

I descend to dust, to earth, its hair pinned with flowers
And so a meaningful tragedy comes to an end
comes to an end. The stars sing gloriously in the western sky
rain blows on my epitaph
spring dies in silence

I open my arms to hold you, stars
I am the night, the endless void

How does spirit ascend?
Eternity is a cloud rising behind the peak and sitting quietly
Smiling at sadness, I ask aloud
Who, who taps on the sinking earth?
When the evening breeze comes and no one's on the narrow path
the leaves whisper
Sunshine's love
has turned into a night crowded with nightmares

Who are you, then, Glorious Singer?
Midnight sleeps, in harmony with deep forest oblivion
You startle yourself, gnaw yourself
Yet who are you? The vast river surges beyond the horizon

Last summer rushes by, moss still thick on the boat
Time covers your radiant face
with gray hair, wrinkles, and doubts
Lifting the drapes, I see you in front of the apple orchard
caressing your beautiful skirt
As for me, stars of May
I descend to earth, its flowered hair . . .
I cross the river in rain

1962

# The Season of Falling Flowers

Standing like this, standing in the rain
a black shadow, without meaning
waits for the long alley to be destroyed, emptied
waits for transient melancholy
It is you, fine dust of my century, who are sad

Fog drifts over misty streets
someone hurries past
each withered streetlight
A rusty ax, the shadow
cuts through silence, silent memory

The suspended haze falls
the land of wind and rain is comfortable
I imagine a rainstorm passing over the mountain
bringing down a few beech leaves. Human hopes
for millennia, stars fall on the land of wind and rain . . .

This world is frail
Walking by myself late at night, along lonesome red walls
The century's mud is deeper and deeper
At the top of a dark building someone
picks up a familiar lantern

1962

# On the Cliff

Then we came to the cliff, sunflowers in bloom everywhere, and
        lay down, startling a partridge returning early
I pointed to the distant mountains and said, "Look, the clouds
        spring water dripping. Just listen to the woodcutters"

All day long we listened to the sound of woodcutting
        The season just begun, forests dense and deep
Who would walk through that magnificent palace
        among a thousand Roman spears and columns
        watch wild wolves take human form
        and sail the sea to reach a golden
    shore?
           When the tide
    comes in, you get a little homesick

You smiled and said, "But we're lying here on a cliff
sunflowers blooming everywhere
thinking of nothing but how to grow old quietly
listening to woodcutters in the distance
spring water dripping through layers of rock"
We were high on the cliff, in each other's arms
lighting a fire, hunting, bathing, growing old

1963

## Strawberry Fields in Summer

The diggers rest under a tree
whose shadow shifts to the east
An orchid-picking man climbs
a broken snow-white precipice. In the distant forest
seemingly growing in the previous century
birds chirp loudly in a cascade
that knows no seasons
I sit in a cabin and watch over
acres of strawberry fields—
acres of sweetness!
Summer's love is congealed
into a valley full of juicy redness

And the sunshine turns whiter and whiter
the cicadas more annoying
as their resounding echoes
are touched with primordial nostalgia
But the valley of juicy redness
is no longer the strawberry fields of our past

1963

# Horse Stables in Light Rain

A row of wind-worn, broken streams outlines
the vast wild of a foreign land
Someone leans against the fence
and tenderly plays a flute
Shallow waters flow across the banana grove
and the sparkling bridge you love

The rainy season leaves veins of boulders
across my body, as I watch a herd of neighing
dappled horses gallop in the drizzling rain
across my dream's withered grove
Leaning against the fence I too am rotting
turning into a fence post—
only more moist
more melancholy

1963

## Autumn Tree

A tree is a symbol always
growing in every dream — it is my love
like the first leaf shadow in early morning where birds nest
I tumble and fall, like the stupid autumn wind
into the tree's depths shrouded in light blue mist

"The leaves on that mountain are so beautiful," you say
"I love those trees . . ." Frost falls and
walks by quietly. There is always a mountain outside the window
a mountain with beautiful leaves — like wisdom
when we quarrel by the riverbank

When you arrive, it is autumn. We go to see the ocean
"Don't think too much. Autumn is here, you should know it
but not think about it!" — you say, looking at the river
where fallen leaves float and a bell chimes elusively
"How can I know it without thinking about it?" The bell chimes elusively

Clouds fly up from the narrow paths, love is a soft song
When we are young and love to smile, we sit under the eaves and
      watch the rain
when the starry sky carries us away on the pale light of happiness
A tree, a symbol
growing in every dream, is my love

1963

# Blue Smoke

Someone comes out of the woods where the wind's died down
A puff of blue smoke rises in the distance
like a song rising to praise
a bleak, ignorant pavilion

Suddenly the smoke clears, we walk under the bridge
think of spring dying young
For a long time we sit wordless before a house
as we watch a man leave the woods
where the wind has died down

Did his eyes take their color from the wind and dust?
When he leaves the woods
he'll see the spring lantern we hang
see you and me sitting, waiting quietly for him

but he'll turn to face—by the city's fresh green walls
you once leaped over—
a white flower with the silence of Time in its hand
reaching from stone steps toward the edge of the well

1963

# Fragment

A wild goose dives in the ancient pool
life sinks within
Nameless ravine, lonely fruit
holding primal peace in the deep mysterious confusion
A man picking flowers among reeds abruptly raises his head
to see a tribe of vultures
A pine fire burns on the clear lot
a small tribe
guarded by a hundred vultures
through misty rain, plagues and superstitions
a tribe of buried totems and taboos
I have seen it once—behind the mountain
across the spring, a tribe in the heart of the jungle
where rebellion and slaughter once took place
Its entire history just an episode of regret

The wind is time sighing, fiery twilight on water
as red as the timeless blood behind the mountain
I lean against a giant tree
that resembles memory, so old
and stern but still
sustaining me, allowing me to sigh
to feel its growth and helplessness
and pass on the legend about a small tribe that once lived

1964

# To Time

Tell me, what is oblivion
what is total oblivion? Dead wood
covered by the decrepit moss of a dying universe
when fruits ripen and drop to dark earth
and summer becomes fall before they rot in murky shadow
when the abundance and crimson of two seasons
with slight pressure break free
suddenly turn to ashes and dust
when the blossom's fragrance sinks into grass like a falling star
stalactites drooping to touch ascending stalagmites
or when a stranger's footsteps pass
in a drizzle through red lacquered arches
and come to a stop at the fountain
solidifying into a hundred statues of nothingness —
that is oblivion, whose footstep leaves a ravine
between your eyebrows and mine
like a mountain grove without echo
embracing primeval anxiety
Tell me, what is memory
if you once lose yourself in the sweetness of death?
What is memory if you blow out a lamp
and bury yourself in eternal darkness?

1964

# In Memoriam: Ch'in Tzu-hao (1912–1963)


Shadows arise from the foothill
along sparse paths lined with white birches
Someone is drinking tea on the riverside balcony
as he listens to the lute
and recalls a poem in midsummer
about Kyoto after cherry blossoms have fallen
the groaning bridge, the clamor on the drunken boat
the velvet beret
You returned from Nice
your face wrinkled by the Mediterranean Sea
like the cracked statue
by the Hsün-yang River
or an orange blossom on the hillside
scattered sunlight glistening at your temples
tree-nestling birds
flying out of sight — on a meteor's homing route
Toward whose arms of a chilly November day do they fly?
Someone is drinking tea on the riverside balcony
Along the sparse paths lined with white birches
shadows arise from the foothill


1964

# In the Midnight Cornfield

1.

In the midnight cornfield
my head on the river's dam, I dream
of spring partridges
taking flight from the bank
like clouds emerging from hills. Twilight
a wine shop's fading banners trail—
sadness from the chimney of a paper mill
reflected in the brass stand mirror
"My eyes are dim, love is like
a napalm bomb" burning away
your arms, your shoes, your book of fairy tales
In the midnight cornfield
you lay your head languidly
on the chilly river's dam, always thinking
of a city where golden apple trees have died, our city
On a snow-drifting, wine-sipping winter night
someone knits a pair of wool socks for you
and wipes coffee stains from the candle stand
The gesture of an aged hand
a farewell song
Your dagger, your dagger
your water bag, your water bag

2.

Or on the streets after the shops have closed
on the revolving city walls
a bell is ringing
On a distant island, the bell rings
while you sit reading a letter
and listen to the motor's sound

Well water

churns your shadow

and breaks subterranean stars and clouds

"My eyes are dim, flowers fall

on my night-dreaming bed, my eyes . . ."

Many spring lamps

many banished rainy nights

thinking about Dryden's *All for Love*

on the bookshelf by the window

footprints in the yard, the corner of a shirt, brass bells

He is a wild goose of no return, dust of no return

that flaps up and falls

a window that opens and closes

1965

# A Verse of Ten Lines: Subtle Fragrance

They sip wine, apples in the autumn sun
scattered smoke fills your yard
I look around: a braid of lonesome wind
tugs at a branch of bamboo leaves
dips into the lake's heart where a tiny boat swiftly disappears

Clothes are twilight, clothes are the brilliant sky
The gesture of walking barefoot on water, isn't it
the intoxication of sunset before departing?
Waves chat about a legend with the evening breeze:
a lotus in the prophecy

1967

# Screen

First, the wall's particular mood
maturing behind warp and woof of satin and paper
like a crop anticipating autumn
an allusion reaches from the painting on the screen
transmitted through a teapot
snagging with a smile
knocking over landscapes and butterflies
in swift vehicles and

sojourns at inns. Forlorn
guilty, packing, a familiar tune
Don't know the mood when the sun sets and dew falls
I paint my eyebrows
while you head for the wine shop

1967

# Weaving

There is a fast-growing forest
ice cold as if from beneath a thousand fathoms
When thunder roars
it swirls and churns and stirs the air like schools of fish floating on water
We live in the fishes' fins, starlight and bright sunshine
We sisters weave
recite a book on weather written by a traveler —
we have no weather

The record of a cloudy day is often prettier than
a battle over a city. They talk about
heavy clouds shrouding date trees
fatigue, hope for spring, et cetera
The sisters weave exotic cloth while they
carefully recite spring's seven, six, eight characteristics —
but they forget the very next day, for
there is a fast-growing forest . . .

1968

# A Sequel to Han Yü's "Mountain Rocks," a Seven-Character Poem in the Old Style

1.

I discuss painting with a monk in the monastery. When day breaks
my feet are wet, my clothes cold, but I think only of
dancing bees among gardenias
women sitting or lying down
behind bed curtains rising or falling, and scholars
scuffling on the edges of brush, ink stand, and classical texts
discussing the Hsuan-wu Gate Coup
Facing the moon I ponder the poetry of Han and Wei
in oblique rhymes; my indignation is more nihilistic
than my host's face

though I have to climb Mount Heng, meet the god of Ch'u
face plantain groves brushed clean by rainstorms. My so-called ambition—
muddy like the South of my exile
When I drink wine, an elusive snake shadow frightens me
When I sing, I imagine amnesty coming soon

2.

I discuss painting with a monk in the monastery. Before I blow out
        the lamp
I suddenly recall willows and
rapids flowing by my ear, teaching me
to be a free spirit like the young Li Po, dedicated to swordsmanship
        and alchemy
Is love just gold hairpins, gauze gowns, and satin slippers?
My schooling is swamp stench and
courtly confusion
I love the round fan
and flitting fireflies

But why write poems for my wife when there's nothing like Tu Fu's
      Fu-chou incident?
All I can do is cross the river and face ten rounds of pine
find a seat on the top floor of a wine shop
wait for a wandering zither player
and fake a hangover
I should not have brought Han rhyme-prose
but I love Ssu-ma Hsiang-ju best

1968

# Prophecy

We are about to enter the chaotic and spasmodic
pleasures of life: winds and rains
twitching rivers running in the four directions
of body and limbs
clamor and peace exploding at the same time
This is the last formation
We cut through it with ease, as sunset cuts
plump pomegranates. To be plants and trees, insects and fish
the direction of a bridge, shoes
sleeves, footprints

Once you reformed like the cultured T'ang Dynasty
and I was your evolution:
the burning Five Dynasties
(A hill undresses beyond the shallows
and tests the water's temperature)

When the season escapes
do you recognize the orchard's call?
In the sound of a startled ax
we are about to enter
the pleasure of life as trivial
and transient as a waterfly

1968

## A Touch of Rain (Ars Poetica)

Moisture on the nape
expands as it rises from my waist
hair is the forest's
climate—
mossy wilderness
a bird flies across
fan's fibers
its shadow of feathers
merges into horrible immensity
your sleeve
a tomb in early spring
breaks hinting at
a certain birth:
first a freshly mounted ink splash
soon
sad and enraged
a warrior rushing toward me

1968

# The Second Renunciation

Still the sound of reed catkins
grinds with ripping
force over a cup of remaining wine, streets aslant
This return did not meet the winter month of drifting wind and snow
Where the bell chimes, a flock of crows arrives
to ask about an untimely death at the Buddhist monastery. Yes

in my memory you are a collapsed stone Buddha
You still smile, but brambles grow like enticing potted plants
behind your ears, under your arms. You were muddiness on the South
     Mountain
born of chance kneading, returning to green moss even now
you have enjoyed centuries of fragrant incense, the midnight wooden fish
Monastic scandals constantly brought before your eyes
You are no god—

They say I committed murder for you
must've been before I went over the pass
and now I've forgotten . . . or only vaguely recall
when I escaped, a floating cloud saw me off to the mountain's joining
when I left, he still sat on the peak with his flustered face . . .
His dejection at my departure was caused by drunken sickness and
     autumn melancholy
and at that time you just stood coyly in the sound of bells and drums
gazing down at a few praying men and women
waiting for me to return, dig wells, grow vegetables for those greedy monks

1969

# Chi-tzu of Yen-ling Hangs Up His Sword

I always hear the mountain's lament
At first I traveled on purpose; how can I explain
lack of concern for so many reunions and partings?
Forget it. For you I dance
with eyes closed. Rustling
reeds in water, chill
of the crescent moon, and
sound of beating clothes in a dusky distant land
trails close behind my shadow and mocks
my rusty swordsmanship. This forgotten scar
on this arm is still there
When I drink enough wine, it glows
as red as flower petals along the riverbank

You and I once sat withering
under the scorching sun:
a pair of drooping lotus stalks
That was before my journey north, when
summer's threat most grieved me. And
the delicate songs of southern women!
Like needle and thread, they stitched and joined
making me draw sword from scabbard
and promise to give it to you on my return . . .
Who would guess that northern ladies, the glorious rituals of Ch'i-Lu
and endless chanting
of the Songs would convert me
into a dawdling Confucian . . .

Who would guess I'd put away my sword?
(People say you kept calling
calling my name, and doing that
you died)

The bamboo flute's seven holes darkly retell

my disillusionment upon reaching China's central plains

In early days, archery, horsemanship, saber and sword

meant more than the arts of rhetoric and debate

After the Master struggled in distant lands

Tzu-lu's violent death and Tzu-hsia's appointment at the court of Wei

we all scrambled for places in great lords' houses

I set aside my sword

tied up my hair, chanted the Songs

and acted like an eloquent scholar


The Confucian scholar!

He cut his wrist in the darkening

woods by your grave—from now on

neither swordsman nor scholar

Perhaps the blue glow of my precious sword can

brighten you and me on this lonely autumn night

You died longing for a friend

I languish as a hermit

The tired boatman, once arrogant, once gentle

is me


1969

# King Wu's Night Encampment: A Suite

1.

On the fifteenth day of the first month, troops ford the river at Meng-chin

2.

We hear only bells and drums in the snowy field
their incessant clamor, but we
are already wounded
trees are wounded too, keeping soldiers warm. Only
the expedition itself has no pity for the river we will wade
Soldiers are divided into seven lines

When the new moon wanders across the sky of the first snow
we listen to Fung-kao soldiers ready themselves for battle
crying cowardly
with wills embroidered on their collars, after all they'll be
the nameless dead
What about hemp-holding widows and abandoned wives? When spring
watches the commander make offerings at the ancestral shrine
declaring the founding of a dynasty from a pool of blood
rising shakily, ashamed

3.

Do not be ashamed of your eloquent sleepiness
or the fatigue waiting for you at the ford
waiting as you silently board the ship and fall pale into the water
into the water to name a new widow for the western land
Widows
    brew no wine, weave no cloth for the victorious homecoming troops

1969

# Floating Fireflies

1.

Poisonous scorpion fluids and thorny
shadows cover my complexion when the tide ebbs
To the east of the broken bridge, black hair spreads out
Dressed as a tired homecoming man
I pull the oars
and row into what seems an unfamiliar bay

A torn map of the constellations in my pocket
a howling wind
Through the dense foliage I see
my enemy sipping tea after food and wine

2.

This orange-scented village deserves to be
burned down . . . a ribbon of smoke surrounds the ancient well
until frogs croak loudly
We wake up on ashes
birds vanish into the clouds
It is quiet all around

My eroding bones are in an awkward state of phosphorus deficiency
Before and after rain I get
melancholy and homesick. At moments like this
a firefly always flits up from the old mansion's ruined garden
nimbly, shyly
It must be my enemy's
only daughter, my wife, whom I killed by mistake

3.

The story has no ending
Cymbals strike on All Souls' Day
peach trees grow as usual

When sharpening a knife makes me sweat
the hillside turns pale, the river ripples as the boat sinks
the wine sours at the bottom of the jug, tears reflect
a flock of migratory birds in the fresh, familiar frost

My mourners are scattered in distant lands;
some become blacksmiths, some peddle medicinal herbs.

1969

# Rondo: The Snake

A.

A cold weakness swims out of my chest and tangles
on a candle stand. Pensive, I ponder your tattooing art, how it provides our
skin with inexhaustible pleasure. If you once lived
in a land lacking transportation—
like the thirty cities plaguing my body—
endured the humble egg, and bravely
shed the sac to play among rivers and hills in blood vessels and bone joints
then you would have smelled me rotting
You are my putrescent prophet

B.

Magnificent prophet! I am surprised
we have the same accent
and are both vegetarians and awed by astrology
although your crawling modesty mocks
my anemic gaze. Old friend, I'm afraid
I begin as a sparkling test tube
that once held strong acids and alkalis . . .
A rainy night will witness the joy of our reunion
but before I can warm some wine to chase away the cold
you fall wretchedly ill

A.

Sick snake, I want to tell you how lonely autumn is
on holidays he always hunts down bandits in the swamps
his whistling embrace scares away handsome apple tree danglings
With your tenderness and gentle warmth, Snake
I beg you to be his lover's bracelet
His lover is the kind of woman who often loses jade bracelets
cannot embroider or pick fruit, but knows how to collect. After all
coming back quietly, you are still my
last companion—you are my road to the graveyard—
clean, cool, the funeral procession's delight


1969

# Etudes: The Twelve Earthly Branches

## *1. Rat*

Prostrate, we wait
for midnight—shapeless midnight
except for a bell chime
coming like childhood
from three streets away

Turn and pay homage to long-absent Aries
Kneeling like a field sentry in the dark
I advance northward
Louisa, please face the earth god
worship him the way I worship your sturdy shoulders

## *2. Ox*

NNE3/4E Louisa
fourth watch, chirping insects occupy the peninsula I just left
Like Aldebaran, I search the wide open
valley, a bamboo grove on the other side

Hunger burns on combat lines
Fourth watch, the intermittent lights of vehicles
quietly flash
across your raised thighs

## *3. Tiger*

Gemini daybreak. Listen
to the earth's raging tears
Listen, my crawling comrades
unclean melons
Listen, east-northeast and north
exploding spring, incendiary shells, machine guns
helicopters chopping up the morning fog. Listen

Louisa, what does the Persian rug say to you?
What does the Asian mud say to me?

### 4. Hare
Please face east when the Crab
shows an array of autumn hues with its many-legged obscenity
Versatile

My metamorphosis, Louisa, is incredible
Patterns of wilderness embroidered on my clothes
swallow baby girls like nightfall
I slaughter, vomit, sob, sleep
Versatile

Please repent with me toward the east
toward the hares of next spring
running and leaping over streams and death's bedding
Please testify with all the pleasures of your senses
Versatile

### 5. Dragon
Lion in the west (ESE3/4S)
Dragon is the occasional East in legends. Now
we can only define a constellation of ecstatic groans
with complete nakedness

East southeast south, Louisa
you who bleed profusely
and suffer so much
are my most allusive
bitterest
secondary star
in the constellation of the Leech
that I define

### 6. Snake
Or leave me with your dew-drenched morning flowers

## 7. Horse

Louisa, the wind's horse
gallops along the shore
Provision was once a rotten shell
I am a nameless water beast
lying on my back all year long. Libra at noon
in the western hemisphere, if I am overseas . . .
in bed, cotton sways on the brimming plain
Libra hangs over the corpse-floating river of lost dignity

I hold the distorted landscape
with my groin. A new star rises from the south
Can my hair and beard be heavier than a shell, Louisa?
I love your smell as you kneel toward the south
like a sunflower moving with time
longing for an unusual curve, oh Louisa

## 8. Ram

"I'll be your fullest winery"
In the afternoon Capricorn sinks into
the shadow of the old continent. High like Taurus at fourth watch
I suck and press the surging vines

Surging vines
the harvest flute slants west
Is Louisa still feeding doves on the porch?
Slanting to the west, poisonous stars
please cover me with her long hair

## 9–10. Monkey-Rooster

Another dashing arrow
45 degrees oblique:
the equestrian archer falls, embracing an armful of moonlight

Rise, rise, rise like the monkey, please
I am a weeping tree by the river

the hesitation of Capricorn
The sun has set to the west

*11. Dog*
WNW3/4N
Fill me with the water of the seven seas
Din at first watch ambushes a square
a drizzling rain falls on our rifles

*12. Boar*
Louisa, please hold me with all the tenderness of America
accept me, a fish of wounded blood
You too are a shining fish
rotting in a polluted city. Louisa
please come back to life in the olive grove
and lie on your back for me. Second watch
a dewy olive grove

We have forgotten so much
A steamboat brings back my poisoned flag
The eagle hovers like a vulture for latter-day carnage
North northwest and west, Louisa
you will scream
when you find me dead upon my victorious return
lying cold and stiff on your naked body

1970

# Part Two

## 1971–1977

# Winds Chase Through a Snowy Forest

Winds chase through a snowy forest
like cartwheels, playful
teasing each other with fading clamor
On the far side stands an ash that has
never seen the end of snow, but winds
chase through a snowy forest

The sound of stars breaking
the scent of a running brook
the swelling of melons—winds arrange an oracle
for a completely new fatigue
hard and hollow like a bullet shell
A skeleton collapses, so

winds chase through a snowy forest
through specks of frail sunlight
scattered desires, sunken beds
and the darkest weeping willows from last night
Between last night's darkest weeping willows winds
chase through a snowy forest

1971

# Nocturne Number Two: Melting Snow

1.

The canal has fallen asleep
a witness to the season's downfall—
it's futile to try to retrieve it
Spring has rotted, become a fallow night
If not for melting snow as light
as soft yellow down on a robin's neck
this would be our permanent frozen lake

At first it is clamorous
as if the Milky Way overflowed
A hanging bolt of brocade facing the wind chime
Flowing lights turn out to be weapons, but slaughter is
futile too. Then desire swells
beyond containing banks—
till they give in to the flood that inundates

a springlike night

2.

We didn't think a pendulum could break solid night
We heard weeping in the distance. Could it be
the moss goddess remembering
leaping fish and flying birds: summer
buried on the roof? Besides tiptoeing silence
only blood climbs along the moonbeam
At first we thought it was fingers playing
tangling like hair
Strangle him; dying young
is all of love, but growing old is just a sad puff of
fugitive smoke—followed by lukewarm embers

looking up at whispering flames
as they go unconscious, expire in ice cold, then the flood

of a summer-insect night

3.
At last it falls like irresistible
melancholy. Touch it, you wouldn't know
that it's tears — ripe fruit
biting wind, autumn of DNA
Perching crows set the tune. If you don't believe it
sit down and listen with all your sleep

At first I thought
the strings broke in protest against war
in fact it was hunger, three thousand miles of hunger
flapping wings across a night of mounting tension
followed by ubiquitous fatigue
gracing the anticipated harvest: pick a branch or tree at random
listen well as it moistens and floods

an autumn-water night

1971

# Sailing to Ireland

*A terrible beauty is born.*

William Butler Yeats

On Saint Patrick's Day
I pin a shamrock on your door
but executioners' gunshots
come back sooner or later. They are back
when on the first sunny day a breeze
wafts through the decay wild apple trees
have waited for—homesick like Ireland

like an Irish winter night
when God passes through the revolutionaries' graveyard
not knowing how to offer sacrifices to
Major John MacBride, who bled and died for violence
Daffodils are not fully grown
shouts are not suppressed, besides
many arrests are being carried out in the city

In the end they can't wait till Easter
before they pick up my shamrock with a bayonet
and trample it. By then spring's here
clouds play at leisure over the sea
salmon reproduce in the mountain brook
new plays are rehearsed in May
People have forgotten what happened

on Saint Patrick's Day

1971

# Almost Number One:
# Landing at Tokyo Airport on July 7, 1971

Almost every sky
draws a snaring curve
Rain is abundant
meadows look forward to the satisfying protection
of mountain shadows, just as it was before the war

The sea breeds warships
scrutinized closely, they resemble fishing boats
Cherry blossoms et cetera have nothing to do
with transit passengers
but samurai swords are for sale
Some really are from the Shogun period
most just replicas for tourists
Handsome bartenders
speak fluent English, though their pronunciation still
carries the prewar abruptness, obstinacy, and self-confidence
though most of the time it is wrong

1971

## Almost Number Two: Every Summer

*For Wang Wen-hsing and Ch'en Chu-yun*
*in Taipei on August Fourteenth*


almost always the same story

fruit ripens on the hillside
sentimentalism of bees and mosquitoes in music
windbreaks resist the invasion of stars

a simple plot: a woman teacher is murdered
except for black plum wine, handkerchief, cash, and nail file
only a long letter to her bedridden mother

calmest are the rice-seeding twilight clouds rising higher and higher
lifting faces from the water, tumbling over the temple
and hiding there


1971

# Water Music

1.

A dazzling beach, dazzling
makes you think it's snow, but it's only
autumn, deep autumn. If you're not sure
turn around: red leaves beyond the swamps, wild geese flying by
shine on in solitude
the crescent moon about to fall

Cold and quiet, because it's
autumn, deep autumn. If I keep sitting here
waiting
I'm afraid the boats will all withdraw to shore
the dazzling beach
No, it can't be a mistake this time — it is snow

2.

I wait sitting by the surf
most of the footprints from last night
The truth is there's not that much sorrow
but maybe sorrow is the best
excuse. Sandy beach, please watch the ebb and flow
for me as soon as noon is past
Now that autumn is here, stretch, stretch
to the place you should be
Maybe I'll just keep walking on, to
the warm bottom of the sea

3.

Something is burning a short
distance away. Maybe not. The red leaves again —
funerals take place in the small town
always when autumn is deep, when it's very deep

before the snow falls, before it really falls
a few simple, solemn funerals

Those who should die have died quietly before the snow falls
The bells chime

4.
But talking does no good
Love is good, when a bed is as high
as the ocean, when wind chimes sway and
dogs chase on the sandy beach, when moonlight plays
and rocking chairs stop, when the farthest sailboat
passes a red buoy

Music is no good, neither is painting
only the ebbing tide reflected off the skin
comes surging toward our limbs—
only love

5.
Only endless sorrow is good
ancient like ice and snow, novel like shocked
tumbling flying fish, only
Let me name you, let moistness be our witness
I have camped in the river valley, wept
like reeds by May's windy shore
gnawed those olive summer nights
guarded sorrow—only
sorrow is good

Whoever has small hands, let her
be cold, even before a charcoal fire. Whoever dreams
let her cheeks be pale
Weakness is necessary
tears are still good

6.

Blood and joy, elusive pain
Maybe next time we will meet
in the heart of a revolving lake
thinking of something else, completely
dizzy. Maybe death is like this:
rowing a small boat alone
swimming downstream, falling too swiftly
to see the willows by the pier
or hear the lute's story
and the pipe's plea to stay

Like this, falling downstream too swiftly
to remember or regret
Maybe death is like this

Maybe it is. Wild smoke
outside the woods, maybe
it is like this


1971

# Lovesong

When snakes
like pouring rain
indignantly (because a rainbow
unintentionally arches toward turmoil
on the other shore) swim to the storm sitting
in the dark, my tired self
please listen to me, please lean on me
When the watery shore slowly
weakens, fireflies' lights going out at last, when
feathers shine on the immense
moonlight and amorous longing
has become a bitter song
please come to me

Let the smoke that has touched the ground
rise again
Let the boat that has sailed away
never turn back
When the narrow road remoistens, insects
chirp loudly once more and change their forms, when the tea is cold
and tears suddenly spill over your pitiful
long-dry eyes, when azaleas
bloom, persist, and wither again
on your breasts, please come to me

Please listen to me, please lean on me
The flower in your hand, don't let it go
Let tardy evening clouds
worry, let
fear change color
let the single peony hide
under the wind's bedding
Please come to me

1972

# Metaphysics

Hunger is delicious
like a pomelo touched by grieving sourness
Youthful love shuttles and floats
in a sweet-olive garden — clearly the
daughter of stars and fog

The daughter of stars and fog
is so melancholy, so suspicious
like musings born of the night —
after thoughtful refining
sprinkled into a rainy lake

1972

# Theology

Wounds and blood and a rib
a piece of Roman cloth that manifests the Holy Son
That, I hear, is all of their theology
sending the apostles on their way in tears—
no one should turn his head before the rooster crows

The worst-tempered were sent to China
Going out, they always rode donkeys
wine sacks hanging
The Yellow River flooded, but that's all right
It can be used to validate the Old Testament
and as an excuse for alms to help
those heathens who do not believe in Jesus Christ

1972

# Geometry

Such adoration of a perfect naked body
like kissing fish revealing love to
creatures in a convex mirror, at last
hydrangeas by the window wither one by one; at last
Venus peeps in; at last
such a perfect, withering naked body

reflected—with the support of a dotted line
of lingering
dove bells in the afternoon—
on
the sea where you often collide with reefs

       a running pose: ankles and arms
forming equal angles
Such adoration of such a naked body
like the mast rushing to embrace a white sail when wind comes
like gazing shyly at myself gliding over deep water
as if that, too, is delight

1972

# Futile Grass

Looking through dark night, listening to the wind like this
is futile in the end:
at first I thought I'd someday be a potted plant
maybe a companion to the lute, zither, and drum by the fire
or, with luck, even an offering on an auspicious day—
but it's futile in the end

Other plants are happier
some become fodder for horses
some are burned to ashes
buried under the northern snow—
even though that's a little too cold

But it's not right living this way
looking around, listening—
futile grass

1972

# Watch

Yesterday's dandelions are dry
wind chimes always shake before it rains. Who's
signaling to us on the other shore?
In a spring like this, no one will drown
in this quiet neighborhood, nor will
anyone send a boat to the rescue

Something seems missing—
I have the pavilion, the wind, and the moon
even a fisherman's song among the reeds
But I seem to have lost my mood
for watching. Maybe
it doesn't belong to the feathery
sweet grass
or the white birch

Maybe if someone drowns—
wordlessly
I watch a hydroplane
swirling, suddenly feel tired and bored

1972

# We Too Will Set Sail

We too will set sail, with
courage a green so dark it's almost turquoise
through rows of cherry and white birch
when startled waterbirds take off to the north
where coldness squeezes from layers of ice
Six-o'clock's wind sweeps over our arms
when we touch it, bitter as mugwort

The new-fired wine jug is left at home—let it complain
When the vase is filled with water, we realize
we're still the Stone Age
and we too want to
set sail, with courage
resembling a nearly vertical parabola
through decaying songs, pleasant
groans, marks of shoulder-snagging
fingernail, through waterlilies
blooming then wilting

Nails work nervously
a wooden coffin sinks
flying banners droop in fresh rain
will-'o-the-wisps grope through the night

Such a gaunt outstretched palm
its star map cannot be entirely read
(Whether you turn east or west
sadness awaits you
and finds you lost in the end)
Footprints play on the wall
the forest on fire beneath your abdomen. Nails

work nervously. You think to yourself: no wonder
will-'o-the-wisps once groped through the night

Through independent decay
we too will set sail with
a courage so subtle it's almost ambiguity


1972

# Fourteen Sonnets
*Selections*

6.

I want to persuade you with
intermittent softness. At last an evening breeze nudges
your flowing dance dress, moonlight
cannot reach your slanting Antarctic
tranquillity. But I imagine you in a
garden of floating fireflies
listening to night birds flapping on the erect snake god
a sad naked body
is more touching than a camellia
Tranquillity
And I want to embrace you with
the eternal moment, like fine snow drifting on
burning power lines
but you are my last night beyond remembrance

7.

Moonlight sits on my body
in a canal seven feet under my bed: a gentle collision—
if not Van Gogh's self-burning sun, it must be
floating weed and
restless fish. Moonlight sits on
the silent head of a drum bridge, peeping at

our many-limbed baby whose
growth, adventures, and death
take place in hard breathing and groans—at this moment
the sound of a boat gliding across still water
is my upturned face
a row of volcanic islands exploding in turn
and falling on a Dutch night

14.

I am tired—
like a pear tree whose fruit has dropped
Only bloody light and shadow
connect the lonely moon and stars
But I see no wandering ghosts
weeping under my skin
In the misty land
seasonal rebellions are repressed
and they say harvests are good this year and
the dams in no danger of breaking

They say this is how a beautiful age
is born in our perfect embrace
I don't know how to plead:
Oh, Hell, please send snow for Heaven

1973

# Kao-hsiung, 1973

The form of this ship is determined solely by its content; the color
of the harbor by Banner Hill, the wind's direction by feeling, the
fidgety heart by the conversions of latitude and longitude.
Thinking so, standing to have my picture taken in the free-trade
zone, I suddenly see a drizzling rain gather from all directions—
swifter than fatigue, a feeling of shame cuts through my sick
chest.

A senior harbor staff member politely recalls how when he first came,
the color of the harbor was determined by war, its form by
Banner Hill, the tide by the wind. His accent indicates he's a
descendant of a North Fukienese family, his speech interspersed
with English terms. Such fine upbringing, they say, is rare
among the older generation of the harbor staff. "Shanghai has
become shallow from Huang-p'u River sediments," he says, "just
like Taiwan's Deer Harbor." "It has declined," he says, "therefore,
Kao-hsiung is the largest Chinese harbor."

Kao-hsiung in the afternoon, its heavy humidity begins to evaporate.
The form of the ship gradually disembodies, waste oils floating
on the water, a clear spell dries the freight on the dock. We walk
along the railway, sometimes standing straight to have pictures
taken. The senior staff member still politely explains to us the
procedures of freight loading and operation, his speech
interspersed with English terms. Suddenly a shower comes, all
thirty-five thousand female workers leaving work at the same
time—but swifter than fatigue, a feeling of shame cuts through
my sick chest.

1973

# Bonn, 1973

1.

The river pales in the bell chime
stars extinguished at the steeple tops
humidity gathers in Beethoven country
Four o'clock in the morning. Don't know
if the fasting woman is awake
(She seems to be protesting against
a certain regime.) City strings
are silent. Fury is no longer
the theme; except for fog in the square
only a shrill, intermittent bugle sound

2.

Compassion full of trills, shorter than
the potted pansies on the windowsill
in Beethoven country in summer
embraces, layer upon layer, and strikes
the fasting woman
(*Freiheit oder Tod*)

That's true
Past nine o'clock in the morning
an Italian bartender tidies up the benches
sets up plenty of sun umbrellas in front of the doorway
A few bell chimes, and pedestrians
walk around brick and rock piles
lean over to watch the subway under construction

3.

At last they realize
how distant Berlin is—
since the war, tank tracks have turned

to a system of fallow buckwheat fields
People still enjoy the freedom to write letters
but on holidays
most of them go north to Holland
or leave the Rhine
and enter the more hearty Bavarian mountains

The afternoon oak grove
buries a completed Schumann


1973

# Elegy

Can't bear to shed tears before the dusky window
for I'm afraid the twilight beyond the window
does not really suit you
(buried under starlight of
silent moss) and I, I hesitate
like a river that has lost its direction
hesitating into a swamp

Sadly the skin's wasteland
spreads at four o'clock in the afternoon
Shaken-off snake vines
green fruit on the ground
woods that have burnt sinking
in eternal geology
to be investigated by posthumous raindrops
sadly searching in the unbearable dusk

Seems the sun's shadow always calls and chases
over the bed, seems
the sounds of nails and boards were once
love and funeral preludes
(You are buried under starlight of
silent moss.) Rising tides
surge toward the dock where I wait
as if you were saying, Let's go to the wasteland
where beautiful prophecies are like thistles
(you are buried under starlight of silent
moss), a small sensitive plant
and hair is today's wind and rain. You asked me
to guess the smell—
wind chimes of June
chrysanthemums of September

1973

# Let the Wind Recite

1.

If I could write you
a summer poem, when reeds
spread vigorously, when sunshine
swirls around your waist and
surges toward your spread
feet, when a new drum
cracks in the heat; if I

rocking gently in a skiff
riding down to the twelfth notch
could write you an autumn poem
when sorrow crouches on the riverbed
like a golden dragon, letting torrents and rapids
rush and splash and swirl upward
from wounded eyes; if I could write you

a winter poem
a final witness to ice and snow
the shrunken lake
the midnight caller
who interrupts a hurried dream
takes you to a distant province
gives you a lantern, and tells you
to sit quietly and wait
no tears allowed . . .

2.

If they wouldn't allow you
to mourn for spring
or to knit
if they said

sit down quietly
and wait—
a thousand years later
after spring
summer would still be
your name—
they'd bring you back, take away
your ring
and clothes
cut your hair short
and abandon you
by the edge of the enduring lake—
then at last you'd belong to me

At last you'd belong to me
I'd bathe you
and give you a little wine
a few mints
some new clothes
Your hair would
grow back the way it was
before. Summer would still be
your name

3.
Then I'd write you
a spring poem, when everything
begins again
So young and shy
you'd see an image of maturity. I'd let you shed tears freely
I'd design new clothes and make a candle for your wedding night

Then you'd let me write
a spring poem on your breasts
in the rhythm of a beating heart, the melody of blood:
breast images and the birthmark metaphor
I'd lay you on the warm surface of the lake
and let the wind recite

1973

# Partridge Sky

1. Evergreens
The lawn's not too wet
stars fill the pond
we haven't lost our way
The smell of flowers comes not from the ground, but
gently
from your shoulders

Where my hands fold
a cloud darkens
A cool stream of air flows by
deep evergreen trees

2. Sleeves
We start to drink
when the night fills
four sleeves seeking warmth in each other:
we are the confused wutong trees

We start talking about the sound of wind and snow
and the soundless sound. We listen in winter to
the album whose label you can't remember
Dry twigs hoist
a languid dream up to the window

"I know how to love"
we start to drink, "and have been
hoping for love to come"

3. Waterbird
Like a boat resting in the heart of a windless lake
we rest on a cloud between the sides of the boat

Though there's no wind, our still boat sways with your breath
on the heart of the windless lake

Years have gone by, years
of love—the bottom of the boat is filled with
green moss and shells
In the heart of the windless lake
you have not languished completely
still blushing slenderly
like a waterbird in the setting sun

4. My Clinging Vine
You untied your hair and gown
facing the ruins where chrysanthemums bloomed
and I looked up to the gods
How earnestly you died
turned round and round, tangled
became my satellite
my clinging vine

Even then you understood
how bleak and
remote I am, and how
airy and lost
you are

5. Chrysanthemums
If you had known
that love is the mixed scent of red persimmon and
mint in a book of poetry
then there would be no need
to shrug your shoulders and say "next time"

Why don't you take off the silk and
just leave the necklace and earrings on
when vehicles grind through the water-puddled alleys

their sounds getting farther and fainter
when the desk clock starts shaking our
time, chrysanthemums closing and falling on pillows
spreading out—
why don't you spread out too?

6. Riverbank
Spreading out like this is good
Intermittent musical notes
eyes are the lanterns
of the Decadents, body hair the
prairies where the Crusaders camped

Lingering clouds in the limbs
stars rise to the forehead
the moon immersed in water
on the abdomen a giant flower
the sound and
shape of dripping from the eaves, twitching blood vessels
and crumbling bones

Another warmer riverbank
sees us sitting fearfully
leaning on each other

1974

# Manuscript in a Bottle

The west is where the sun sets
over the cypresses, waves
on the shore, but I know every breaker
begins at Hua-lien. Once, a confused boy
asked the distant land:
Is there a shore on the other side?
Now I'm on this shore, that's the other shore, and I see only
twinkling stars

Only the stars
shine on my haggard dejection
as I eagerly ask if the surging waves
miss Hua-lien's sandy beaches

I gather it takes ten summers
for a wave breaking on Hua-lien's shore to turn around
and reach this shore
Surely, with its resolve to plunge back into the water
it takes shape the moment it turns around . . . suddenly
another wave comes in
rolling peacefully onto the lonely shore

If I sit listening to each wave
and observing its shape—
a sketch of my future—
the small one on my left
could be a newly hatched roe
that one there, medium-sized
is probably seaweed, and the
big one in the distance may be a flying fish
tumbling in the fire of a summer night

As a wave rushes to
the lonely shore, I wonder what
would be the best decision
Maybe I should be a breaker
swiftly reversing in the backwash
plunging into the peaceful sea
and brimming over the sandy beaches
of Hua-lien

Yet, when I set my foot in the water
a minuscule addition in weight causes the level to rise
and wet the shore even farther on the other side
and as I walk on, if I submerge myself
seven feet to the west off this lonely shore
will Hua-lien, my Hua-lien in June
start a rumor of a tidal wave?


1974

# River Goddess: Geometry

A.

Coming across the water
she is a goddess. The oars carry the boat along
almost without sound
a white boat emerging
between the pavilion and willows

A goddess is coming, like bell chimes
drifting across the lake
only to disappear in the next moment—
moonlight on her shoulder
frost on the prow and stern

B.

The lanterns mark
her trail along the water
in the lake's grid
every two squares holding a waterlily
She is coming, but she is invisible
She glides closer, but she lingers far away
Who does she wait for on the islet in mid-water?

Each time the lanterns
glide into a square, a waterlily
illuminates the moment
like her approving smile
Weaving in and out of darkness
the boat leaves in its wake a flickering line
between distant pavilion and nearby willows
Is she a goddess? She must be
moving swiftly like a startled wild swan

graceful as a soaring phoenix, her beauty beyond autumn
        chrysanthemums and spring pines
She is coming toward me, but she is getting no closer
The slender oars quietly skim the lake—
a vision beyond mortal reach

C.

Even so
the moon shines on the trees where the goddess stands
with her hair untied. I will think of a new name
for the trees in the moonlight

The boat glides over the coordinates on the grid
She begins to sing softly, like a flower opening and closing in the fog
a fishnet sinking slowly
willow leaves brushed by moonlight
frost falling. The lyric of the song says:

>           I hear the fair lady beckoning me
>           We'll fly away together
>           And build a home in the middle of the river . . .

She is coming, but she is getting
no closer. She lingers
her trail sparkling now and then, each light
a waterlily in bloom


1974

# Untitled Verse in Regular Meter

You give me
a boatload of early summer constantly changing
sliding between lotus leaves
till it finally sinks, falls apart
Aquatic creatures shuttle freely, chattering
past your breasts, arms, waist, and abdomen
they mistake the dead on their backs for coral
and play among weeds of hate
weeds of love, weeds of neither love nor hate
Special fish come later

I give you
bones that have collapsed but not yet decayed
the dawn-insisting darkness in the ravine
You begin to snap and murmur
in search of a frail light
crawling in new ashes
old ashes, ashes neither new nor old
tepid warmth, tepid coolness
your wavering elusive eyes
are the retreating star

1974

# With Hands Behind My Back I Watch Snow

With hands behind my back I watch snow drift to the lake without a sound
In my heart the snow freezes into
a mirror that barely reflects. I think of
the image of a dark lacquered dragon around the rim
maybe now faded and chipped
maybe beyond anyone's recognition, but I
have always loved its lofty, regretful
lines, and am anxious to take the mirror down and wipe it clean

With hands behind my back I watch snow pile higher and higher on
     the slope
On my forehead ice congeals into an ancient, solitary cliff
a stiff precipice forbidding the moonlight to climb
though it tries again and again
(Winter birds perching on the trees can't help chuckling)
Look, it fell into the lake
a broken crescent; it would take fifteen days and nights
of stumbling and climbing to make itself swollen and
foolish again. It's been like this since antiquity

With hands behind my back I watch the loving snow on the plum tree
put a coat on winter branches that will soon be part of my painting
as ice grinds the inkstone with its fingertips
According to the composition and brushwork of court paintings
a mere plum tree
offers nothing special, until we
abstract it, emphasize its expected
flourish and decay, symbolizing life and death. Even so
it is still praised as the only spirit that can survive

With hands behind my back I watch the snow drape
over someone's window. Ice melts in the groin

as if feet were thrown through a thin layer of

snow as they crossed the chilly silence

Only a spasmodic cry

rises between singing and cursing

to the same depth as the feet. Haggard, I turn to gaze at

a pot of red flowers blooming in profusion by my clean bed

1975

# Zeelandia
### *T'ai-nan, Taiwan*

I.

The enemy side has entered the muggy droning of cicadas
I look up from below stone steps; dense broadleaf trees
open into a bed of wind—
giant cannons have rusted. And I don't know how to calmly ravish
her new blue flowered dress
in the history of stampeding gunsmoke

A bright expanse delights me
like a European sword boldly piercing through
a fallen torso. We go up the steps
drum in the troops, but when I
loosen her row of twelve buttons
I find what welcomes me still are her familiar
cool breasts asserting a birthmark
Enemy ships deploy on the sea
we sweat and get out of the rain

2.

Enemy ships are busy preparing for attack at dawn
we sweat as we set up defenses
Two pillows build a cannon mount
cicada droning fades away, the subtropical wind
churns into a swaying bed
To begin with you are a water beast from another land
so smooth, so clean
your limbs more slender than ours

Your accent sounds crisp too
it's a cry for help when ramparts crumble
and false as a dried-up well

Whenever I bend over, I always hear your
endless empty echoes

3.

The giant cannons have rusted, gunsmoke
vanishes in history's broken pages
but I, worried, caress your waist
Once more the row of glossy green broad-leaf trees
waits for me to lie down and name it slowly

Seen from the bell tower
it's one of your slanting pendants
each pearl is a battle
bullet holes from fierce fighting all over the trees

In my embrace of sulfur smoke, Holland's body
rolls like a windmill

4.

Counting in silence, I slowly loosen
the twelve buttons of the new dress
In Zeelandia sisters share
a dress that falls off easily in summer: the wind comes from the strait
and teases the open butterfly collar
where I thought I'd discover an archipelago of spices. But who would know
what appear before me still are
those cruel mint-scented breasts. Isla
Formosa, I've come to lie on
your bed of cool wind. Isla
Formosa, I've come from far away to colonize you
but I have surrendered. Isla
Formosa, Isla
Formosa

1975

# Song of Gray Hair

In the beginning I thought time was a pool of
stagnant water stained with civilization's sadness
Night fell, spring chill set off an explosion in my flesh
floods rose and fell. At last, I
entered the Paleolithic Age of hunting

In my dream I searched for a blue mountain faint as a lock of hair
where the pigeon disappeared. When the wind stopped I saw
a group of women, all in black, walking, then sitting
in a circle, exchanging strange gestures
mysterious gestures, expressing nothing but
grievances against the wars, which were
all excuses, they said, for mȳ heroic entrance
into the Neolithic Age

A reckless man set the mountain on fire
in the ashes we discovered copper
I took some to forge man-slaughtering weapons — first cutting off
their ears so I could become an arrogant, braggart king
the rest I gave to officials so they could make mirrors —
to impress their women so they no longer had to comb their hair by
        the river —
but I won't go into that

Let me tell you about another one-eared good-for-nothing
To avenge the shame he suffered from a bloodstained shoulder
he spent ten years on a mountain, mining and extracting
before he discovered the hardest substance of all
Grinding it, hammering it, singing to it with wine
he fashioned an icy, glowing sword. With that I entered
the Iron Age of martial flourish

But then I began getting old
During my worst years of decline
missionaries came from the West and presented me
with a glass goblet, a crystal vase
and a mirror that shamed me
each time I counted the rebellious gray hairs on my temples

1975

# Yin-Yang and the Five Elements

*Metal*
Like the sound of metal objects bumping one another
tumbling from the bedroom where we meet but remain strangers
That familiar lamp was once
someone's face; beyond that
a huge mirror keeps telling your stories

I can't believe that besides slaughter and
despondency, this primitive mine, once taking form
is a necklace leaning to the left when you
sigh softly to the right. I don't know
how to describe the jade bracelet you just bent down to pick up

*Wood*
Even though we can't cultivate the land like spring rain
or analyze forest trees like a summer sunset
I will approach you with the abundance of autumn
A snow-laden purple bamboo is your yearning song
in the deep of the night I choose it, I choose you

I know you are a lantern boat going against the current
but I sit alone, musing at the head
of the torrent, waiting with the melody of growth
hurrying a woman on her way to a rendezvous. My moist
forest, if you set fire to it, will belong to you

*Water*
I dream that you traverse a long sandy beach
with a long letter in your pocket. My window
half open, velvet curtains sway like
abdominal muscles—when they meet, they search for the truth of the senses:
that must be because you heard me calling

Nothing else. I watch from the tower
in a rainstorm but cannot witness
your twitching on the pillow between laughter and tears. Time
is nothing but the distance between pistils and fruit
I test you with the metaphor of thunder and lightning

*Fire*
A series of taps on my door, I hear them clearly—
it is absolute thunder and insistent lightning
I want to close the window that faces the sea, but
my hands seem covered by the seeds of lilacs
sinking with a certain weight in spring rain

Temperature spreads around lips
encouraging the tongue to play, and rises high
in this season of panic. A precise pink drop
of mercury . . . in a moment we will burn
when you offer seeds of fire from your shifting eyes, when you . . .

*Earth*
Under the navel, where all rivers and streams
diverge and flow vaguely southward—
my land is still a new continent
with so many lakes and reeds, familiar to you
seemingly strange to me

I test you with my blind horse tightly bridled by ten fingers
traveling over prairies and hills. One evening I
carried twilight on my back to your window; the lamp
I searched for was once your face
A huge mirror keeps telling, telling you stories.

1975

# Nocturne

I walk along the river
my lingering midsummer illness heavy as a wet coat
I don't know if I was injured by the flowers
or damaged by the wine

But I am a traveler who cannot take a hard journey
fearful of the stars and their ambivalent directions
fearful of tree shapes, sounds of birds
spreading their wings, and tiptoeing animals
And I am so
afraid of the night

(The night falls impatiently
Do not sing dirges)

Dejected and faint of heart
I silently count the night's footsteps
in its slowness there is the insistence of solidity
The truth is, sensing through my lingering midsummer illness and my
skin, I find the night so hesitant

The night falls hesitantly
Please listen to my dirge

I cannot stand the automatic explosion
of a floating mini-universe
in inexplicable silence. The thundering sound quickly
destroys the resistance of my flag-hoisting fortress
Arrows, bee stings, tongues of fire, bayonets . . .
(I know of course) if I insist . . .
But I am decadent, my lingering midsummer illness
heavier than wet clothes. I don't know if I was injured by the flowers
or damaged by the wine, or if it came from

the torrential rain leading to the flood

in my memory—

I can't bear its coldness

I can't bear its heat: a boundless

forest burns in my chest

swamps boil, summer miasma

spreads to my flustered limbs, wind and frost

tumble behind my eyeballs . . .

Lava, trajectories, lightning, steel mortars

spirit vanish in the rising temperature

vision corroded by tears

the endless wasteland calls a blind man's

eloquent wind. When the night falls hesitantly, I walk

along the river

My lingering midsummer illness heavy as a wet coat

I don't know if I was injured by the flowers

or damaged by the wine. Please listen to me

sing a dirge

1975

# Claire de lune

temperature drops rapidly
wisteria still today
after pouring rain a film of frost will cover the earth

                                        wisteria wilting
                            a sad quiet will surround you
when you wake up, find yourself in an abandoned skiff

in an abandoned skiff
the sea will not break tomorrow
full eclipse of the sun, a heavenly dog patrols far away

                                        the sea is sobbing
                                fish and dragon weeping
when you wake up, find yourself in a faded tent

in a faded tent
armor once clanged
at the end of bloody battle, wolves and jackals turned to rocks

                                            arms to dust
                            decayed grass into fireflies
when you wake up, find yourself in a sunken ivory bed

in a sunken ivory bed
body scent is eternal memory asleep
the waning moon, tear scars on the pillow like moonlight

                                body scent like moonlight
                                    you like moonlight
shining on my aging, rapidly dropping temperature

1975

# Solitude

Solitude is an ancient beast
hiding in my jagged rock heart
A stripe on his back that changes color—
I know it's a protective device for his species
Loneliness in his eyes, he often stares at
distant floating clouds and yearns for
celestial shifting and wandering
He lowers his head and muses, allowing the wind and rain to whip
his abandoned ferocity
his wind-eroded love

Solitude is an ancient beast
hiding in my jagged rock heart
When it thunders, he moves slowly
laboriously, into my wine cup
and with adoring eyes
looks at a twilight drinker
I know at a moment like this he regrets
having left his familiar world
and entering my cold wine. I lift the cup to my lips
and with kindness send him back into my heart

1976

# Three Mournful Songs

1.

Your letter says your heart is weak
but still beats night and day
after all still     still
a kind of life     a life
of anticipation

The rainy season is coming to
an end after all. Before it ends
you may as well dream, dream many dreams
(In modern literature dreaming is shameful
but it's real in classical love stories)

What else? Maybe
I should advise you to travel
and see seagulls fly, stay overnight
in an unknown place. Tomorrow I am
going to find an unknown place and stay overnight

2.

That day you came to say goodbye
you sat by the window, rueful
Then the sky darkened. I wanted to make
a few vows
like cherry blossom time

plantains' dense
whispers—maybe you would've liked that
Before I could open my mouth, you tidied your hair
then the sky darkened. "I'm leaving," you said

"anyway it's all useless." In the silence
we heard the woman next door yelling at her dog

her man persistently hammering a nail
They were living. "I am living,"
I said, "though I don't know what for"

3.
At last I understood the meaning
of your letter—I draw a range of blue hills
a grave, a swarm of yellow butterflies
I draw a white birch
butterflies flying up to the birch

Worry makes you old
(though not as much as worry
for your homeland) I disembody gradually but cannot stand
the loneliness when my body is eroded by the wind
You want me to flow, flow into a narrow stream

Someday you can follow the stream
to visit a grave on the hill. Maybe you'll get lost
but you must remember the swarm of butterflies I drew
they'll lead you to a white birch slightly taller than the one
in the drawing. I am here . . .

1976

# How You Feel

### 1.

I think I know how you feel
when dusk fades from the poinsettias
dark night on the roof, dark night patrolling
the roof of dimming red tiles
Your feeling is frost and snow
I test it and feel the tepid warmth
seven fathoms below where there once was a volcano
The volcano is how you feel, I know

### 2.

I think I know how you feel
when dark night disappears from the oleanders
frost and snow on my temples, frost and snow
resting on my temples where wind and rain no longer exist
Your feeling is an icy cliff
I listen hard and hear cuckoos from
ten millennia back when there once was a prairie
The prairie is how you feel, I know

### 3.

I think I know how you feel
when daylight knits a warm scarf
out of reed catkins, for you
a hat and a dress for standing in the wind
Your feeling is clouds and haze
I look hard and see giant
waves where there once was an ocean
The ocean is how you feel, I know

1976

# After the Snow

Bitter cold
after the snow
Coming back from the woods
I can't bring myself to walk
in the garden's myth and poetry. I hesitate
standing at the foot of the silent bridge
There is a light in the house, a broken tune
drifts here and there
a potted winter plum lowers its head
to gaze at its own slender shadow

I hear a sigh
coming from behind the door
someone's reading a book
on dream analysis
The snow has stopped; there must be a fire
in the house—but I am last year's extinguished fire
someone's kindling me, poking me
like a handful of whispering stars

I can't help moving closer
because I hear a sigh
coming to me like plum fragrance
I hear the pages turning—
let me interpret your dreams
I have returned from a foreign land to verify
the rising and falling temperature. If you are
still cold, then put me
in the fireplace and make a fresh fire
for the night

1975

## Forbidden Game 1

Noontime
leaves sway gently outside the screened window
swaying to an ambiance, an incomprehensible romance
(The G string is hard to control, she says, her hair falling to the left)
Head lower, her ring finger presses music from a Granada wind
Chanting the rosary inside the window, a nun raises her head—
a wanderer's horse saunters by in the distance
The horse trots so slowly; she has counted twelve rosary beads
The wanderer vanishes over the horizon. So Lorca says . . .

The papaya trees near the ranch
are rapidly bearing fruit. The noontime air
seems to carry an abundant stillness
Twelve years seem still too—
she's finally learned to control the G string, even
the beautiful timbre of the note

Then I hear, I hear the sound of a chinaberry growing
and at the same time dropping fruit: at first
the span between leaving the branch and touching the ground is short
seven years, twelve years later, it has gotten longer and longer
(We measure it with silken threads of spring rain, but I
can hardly endure the span of separation)
The moment the chinaberry plumbs through the octave
then another moment—a low, bitter dripping sound
one lower than the first, more bitter
than the first

At last it hits the ground. She raises her head
and sees me listening gloomily to the invisible leaves
swaying gently outside the screened window. At noon
a white cat naps on the balcony

Last winter's dried leaves gather before the steps
dried leaves from years ago pile up in my heart
"I've finally learned to control the G string," she says, "like this—"
With a smile, her ring finger presses easily, like a prairie
a Granada wind . . .
The poet opens the door and walks to the intersection. Quiet noon
suddenly a cluster of gunshots, Lorca
is speechless as he falls

People push open the windows to look
knocking over several pots of pansies
Under the fierce sun the prostrate chinaberry is one octave lower
ending a short-lived grand romance in silence

1976

## Forbidden Game 2

In a faraway place, behind the maple grove turning red
a river swells after a fresh shower
I can hear the sound of trout breathing each other in
hear the evening smoke report on autumn's abundance
and desolation. But a serene mood
is louder than all these sounds
more solemn too—in a faraway
faraway place

Allow me to rethink the question of time. "Music"
you say as you lay your left hand on the octave, "is a temporal
art. What about spatial arts?
And combinations of time and space? And . . ."
And the uplifting, ecstatic joy of the union of time and space
and spirit. Sometimes
I can't help facing a river swollen after a fresh shower
after the maple grove and evening smoke
before serenity

Sometimes you can't find my traces
(even if you try very hard), sometimes
night falls slowly on this side of the valley
A bugle echoes through the fortress. I walk a path
leading directly to death and eternal life
You may be able to find it on fantasy's
prairie, on the edge of dream
in tears, in blood

I find it hard, hard to believe this is a dead man's song
floating in a simple, moving legend
accompanying rumor (a bugle
echoes through the fortress): people stand around and listen

till pounding cavalry hoofbeats surround the town
getting closer and closer . . . then the people
innocently disperse

"There is the joy of the union of time and space
and spirit," the poet says
"an uplifting, ecstatic joy"
In a faraway place
a river swells after a fresh shower
and looks serene
But I hear a mood more serene, more sonorous
than any sound, a slight rage real
as a low cry, on the edge of dream and memory
in tears, in blood

How do you forget that reality—
across the preparation of reeds, whispers of stars and trees
homework of the moon and sea—how do you forget a street
some fruit and wine (even
if you can)? I can't imagine
the gunshot that leads to death and eternal life
when I enter the maple grove
turning red, I cannot imagine

this is a dead man's song, floating in
a simple, moving legend
accompanying rumor—
a bugle echoes through
the fortress


1976

# Forbidden Game 3

Try to remember
the great concern in Granada
try to remember your language and pain
green winds and green horses, your
language and happiness—your occasional happiness—
beyond the grove by the awakening riverbank
a donkey's hoofbeats at this moment are louder than wine and harvest

She wishes to talk to you, with multisyllabic words
she wishes to talk to you (with gestures, too)
She inquires about the direction of the church
though this doesn't mean a young person like her
already understands religious Granada
Saint Michael, please protect
this good, curious girl
bring her up

teach her to hear—as she listens to the bell chime—
history's deeper sigh
recorded in an obscure place in the textbook
on the other side of the olive stained-glass window—
the peasants' sweat
the soldiers' blood
Teach her to recognize the row of fig trees on the riverbank
A wind once came from the assembled fortresses
and persecuted a boy who left home on Sunday
(his love as pure as his cap
he could recite Lorca's new poems)
The boy once lay dying under a row of beautiful
fig trees, too soon to shed
a peasant's sweat and a soldier's blood

Teach her to listen and know all this

Then you can give her back to me
a radical heathen
We'll spend the whole winter
studying rhetoric and semantics then
forgetting rhetoric and semantics. We'll
spend the spring traveling
discussing Granada's myths and poetry
in a tavern throughout the night. We'll
do field work and interviews
and together spend the long summer vacation
collecting folksongs and proverbs. And autumn
will find us inside a red-leafed window
wiping away peasants' sweat and soldiers'
blood; the little donkey's hoofbeats will
be louder than wine and harvest

You will love such a good, curious girl
Saint Michael, try to remember
that great concern


1976

# Forbidden Game 4

Chilly sunlight brightens up a gutter
It's so quiet: the residents may be reading morning papers
no exciting news
can destroy this morning's emptiness
Hovering slowly, surviving mosquitoes
trace shiny vectors. There's not even a breeze

I sit at Granada's edge
meditating on the poet's bleeding heart
A guitar leans in a corner of the tavern
in the lingering warmth of last night's fire
I say to myself: "Music is at best
ornamental to the story, so are melody and rhythm"
When the music's lost (for example, now)
the story is still there, the hero still alive
so is the one he said goodbye to
now combing her hair in a flowering garden

If music is really fit for defining love
is love merely ornamental to life?
So I sit wondering, a few gray pigeons on the street
strutting and pecking around. There was bleeding there once
"Love, when it vanishes (for example
this moment, or tomorrow, or next year)
can life go on?" Someone insists
love is the whole of life

Still thinking
I sit at Granada's edge
A donkey comes up from the other end of the street
followed by a bleary-eyed man—
last night he spread six rumors. Yet

"when love vanishes, life can still be
finished out." Delighted, I move toward this conclusion
Heroes are still learning cross-country warfare and demolition
even if he gets killed in a foreign land or only
executed by the cavalry in the morning, the once-leaping
life still lives in a place farther than Granada
the one he once said goodbye to still
combs her hair in a flowering garden

This conclusion satisfies me
as I lift my head to look at the chilly sunlight
brightening up a gutter. I get up from the desk
Someone picks up a guitar in some corner of the house
and repeats a faraway grand romance
Delighted, I walk toward the pecking pigeons
The man with the donkey (last night he'd
already spread six rumors about me)
turns around to beckon me with bleary eyes—
the guitar suddenly stops

a cluster of gunshots . . .


1976

# Not an Elegy

Now as I look back at the misty rain falling on the ferry between
   Hong Kong and Kowloon, I remember someone told me maybe
   your last trip would save you. I think of how you got really
   drunk in Iowa snow—think of it, then forget it. Anyway I don't
   think of you often, so how can I say that I have forgotten you?

That day I walked out of the Humanities College with a friend,
   talking with him about his project of translating modern fiction
   from Taiwan. I ran into a bunch of students who said they were
   going for some Vietnamese food. "In remembrance of a demo-
   cratic country," someone said, "in remembrance." When I went
   back to my apartment, I received the news of your death. Your
   last trip did not save you.

Now I think of the chrysanthemum fields on both sides of the
   Kowloon-Canton Railway, angry that you just died and didn't
   give me another chance to debate with you. We debated once,
   six or seven years ago, with wine bottles and cigarettes in front of
   us, before dawn, in the midst of Paul Engle's corn field.

This morning I went to buy loquats and watermelon. Traveling
   through the underpass I thought of your last trip. I went home,
   drank tea, and brooded, my right hand trembling from having
   carried too much weight. I felt a stream of cold air in my chest,
   I wanted to cry, but how could I cry over a life like yours?

I opened the drawer, took out the English poem you had written in
   1970, and read it out loud. You mentioned Mrs. Gandhi, George
   Orwell, Aldous Huxley, Dylan Thomas. I used to be enchanted
   by your distinguished voice, even more your love for human-
   kind. I loved . . .

I loved your rhythm that resembled a Welsh hill. The wanderer died in New York, the man in your poem died in Taipei, and you died in your own rhythm. Your 1970 English poem has a nice title: "Not an Elegy."

1976

## Asking the Dancer

Can you possibly be a waterlily at dusk at seven o'clock?
When a frog leaps into the lake, can you possibly be
an awakened waterlily, swaying gently
in the twilight, right and left as in an ancient dance
then standing still inside my breath?
Summer dew has not yet reached the lawn
not a breeze, only a single star in the sky
Can you get close to me like the ancient waterlily
but still remain distant across the misty water?
I think you can. I fear you are . . .
even in hair-dense tree shadows
in a quiet alley, when over the fence
an orchard secretly prepares a story dance
expecting the high-pitched flute. At this moment

can you possibly be a hibiscus at eleven o'clock?
When a sparrow is startled awake on its wings
by a falling Buddha fruit, then immediately
pulls back, disappears into night
can you be that hibiscus?
Its mood is also vermilion, capable of
mirroring a traveler's complexion like a foreign dance
something I have never seen with my own eyes
Its air is naturally grand and gentle
somewhere between the Elegantiae and the Greater Odes
glorifying benevolence and satirizing tyranny—
even with light's shifting movement
depicting migrations, battles, and the peace of our ancestors
I believe you can

1976

# Answering the Dancer

This side of waterlily leaves
some excitement and tiredness, we
discuss the directions of summer and autumn winds
The sun shines brightly. This side of waterlily leaves
we observe how birds land on flowers
learn some swinging and balancing skills

This life is distant and long, this life
you only begin to realize
I explain a few common allusions in classical poetry
this side of waterlily leaves. Sometimes I use historical rises and
falls as analogies, or the glory and decay of
natural history; sometimes I use
difficult English terms
sometimes I look at you
in silence

This life is distant and long
you have fully realized it

Tomorrow is a gentle swaying, tomorrow is
an event, beginning, ending. Forever
you alone will interpret this brief moment
interpret the abstract with the concrete, flipping your right hand
using our Buddha's gesture of great benevolence
This is the dance of your life. Allow me
to interpret the concrete with the abstract
I will use no allusions

1976

# Lullaby

To the north of the river where streets twist and turn the most
oh, Emily, at the end of spring when summer's
about to begin, you were born in a world
you were born in a world unfamiliar to me
Lilacs at the ferry by the south shore
roses bloomed at your side, roses bloomed

A church bell was ringing at your side, ringing happily
I insist in an expanse of misty rain
insistent as I am I won't be lost
Emily, let the bell keep ringing
I'll find you as long as the bell keeps ringing
to the north of the river where streets twist and turn the most

To the north of the river where streets twist and turn the most
oh, Emily, behind a faraway cape
reefs and islands guard a city
where you were born in my senses, my complete senses
Seven-colored birds gather on a cherry tree
butterflies fly at your side, butterflies fly

Rainbow in the sky, in the towering sky at your side
On a long road I insist
insistent as I am I won't be lost
Emily, when the rainbow points to your cradle
I'll find you as long as the rainbow points toward you
to the north of the river where streets twist and turn the most

1976

# Folksong

### *On the Fortieth Anniversary of Lorca's Death*

She knocked at the door in spring chill
recounting winter's burning and slaughter
in a snowy wooded field in a border town
She came from far away
an unknown woman with some experience and enlightenment
good at telling sad stories
"How sad," she always said, "those stories of mine"
You listened to yourself cavalierly punctuate, annotate, and comment on
some tangled details of the plot
drawing on your trivial philosophy from dripping eaves
Maybe you can rewrite a few passages into
folksongs, so you thought
as you listened coldly

You took her in generously
gave her some warm clothes
three simple meals
and a basket of needles and thread
But you were suspicious of her stories
folksongs are mistresses you can do without

1976

# Virgil

Long hair spreads out on my left arm
you lay your head on dawn's wind
in my frail worn sleeves
I lay my head on Virgil

You stare at the lamp in front of the window
but I know you are thinking of Rome
Besides the wandering and slaughters in founding an empire
you should remember fine pastoral songs

The wind comes from the golden boughs above
but here a cold forest in light ink
regulates the hermit's heart
I let you lay your head on dawn's arm

I lay my head on Virgil
and hear the burning and downfall of cities
weapons abandoned on plains of morning smoke
a ship quietly waiting on the sea

1976

# Reed Field

1.

It's a chilly morning
In the reed field not too far from
the city, I stand in the wind
imagining you going through crowds—
I'm surprised to find myself enjoying
the wait, but I say to myself
this waiting in the wind will be
my last

I count the potted plants on the balcony
trying to decide the age of the banyan tree
I see the morning light strike
a winter chrysanthemum at an angle
As you are walking through the crowds
the air congests with
glittering anxiety
I want to stop you or
hurry you, but I cannot see you

I sit down and run my hand over a teapot
feeling the delicate lacquered phoenix wings
and the warmth behind the allegory
contented with the peace of my age
I discover that the doorbell image
appears in the Romantic period, printed in a chapter
of a book already covered on the exam
I turn to the last few pages
on structuralism and doubt
if my inductive method suits
you. I only know I cannot

force you to accept my subjective conclusion
and so decide to let you express yourself

2.
I decide to let you express yourself
and make your own judgments. I will not
question your choices anymore. Time
is a river, now dark, now bright
those on the bank cannot question
the surge and fall of the light

I should even
learn knitting from you
how you knit while carrying on a conversation
looking sweet and relaxed
Only your smile reveals
a touch of uneasiness — sometimes
the needle pricks your index finger
wound with thread. Yes, like me you
try to act calm but cannot help
being distracted

It's a chilly morning
We pretend to be happy as we pass
the lukewarm teacups. I pretend
not to know that when the tea cools
the phoenix also turns cool
I pretend sadness belongs to the future
not to the present, to this moment, though
the sun rises higher and higher. In the reed field
not too far from the city
we promise each other
unrealistic dreams
of a bigger, happier

world, in a distant
future world

until I hear you crying
the way you express yourself
I know this is not the last time
I'll wait because I love you

1977

# Complete Handicraft

Now is the time for saying goodbye
and languidly revealing what life conceals
The future in the palm of my hand, in my blood
maybe in my memory like a cloud ambling behind a peak
a cloud rising in rainstorm. Please look
at his frosty temples in the red aura of the candle on the table

Give me all the illusions, you can keep the reality
I will take away the frogs' croaking in the night and the golden sun of
    the day
Sounds will disappear on the road. What about colors?
Colors will weave profound thoughts
but I don't think sounds will disappear on the road
they'll make trimmings for thoughts

I will possess complete handicraft
on cold nights I will lay my head on it. But I won't have
dreams, will you?
Forget it. The gold banner trimmed in blue
is flying on a prairie in a distant land
a stray wild goose in the dusk

1977

# On the Death of an English Literature Professor

I hear it was early in the morning on a coastal island, the most difficult
moment; his death enters my limited consciousness like a sinking island
And I, because of his death, have located the island
southwest of dream, northeast of reality—the bell tolls slowly
tolling for Arthur Oberg, for you, for me

I still remember how under a dripping oak tree—he in a trench coat
reminding me of the European War—Arthur and I discussed
the Metaphysical Poets. He had a pair of big
shiny eyes, the rest beyond description
And that most difficult moment early in the morning on a coastal island—
I turn to the map to look for the time and place of his suicide

Near the floating dock
against the rising sun
I hear
he left behind a long poem

1977

# Part Three
## 1978–1985

# Rondo Number Two

Worried, unable to bear the burden—
the familiar look of a stranger
You may think my anxious eyes
are gentle and earth is the color of my face
You say once you decided to be a bystander

Bystander? Let me guess:
yesterday you drifted along the east coast
crossed the northern lake and went south
with snow on your shoulder-length dark hair
You traveled alone to the mouth of a quiet river

West of the sea, south of the lake, the mouth of a quiet river
You dust off the snow and decide not to leave
Facing the mirror, you dry your hair and think
how can this haggard person be me?
Don't look back on all that is past

Let me guess all that
let the snow fall, let the bell—when
festivals come, outside the woods
intermittent in a morning square—chime
At last, spring illuminates your country

You leave spring days in your open hands
in books and albums. But
after that I can guess no more
Railings, long bridges, hard-to-read maps and charts
a few memories, a few burdens

Let memories be left behind and listen to me:
the look is familiar but it would not admit loneliness
at times it is gloomy but not sad
Actually I'm still optimistic
don't know what you are worried about

1978

# Dying Young

You listen to tiny fish splashing
look at glittering sunlight on a spring river
A breeze blows through drooping willows on the banks
wild strawberries climb over old moss on ancient cliffs
happy lizards come out of hibernating caves
to see the brave new world with wild trailing smoke—
a world taking shape in ignorance. You listen
to your own faint weeping
the sound of a leaf prematurely turning yellow

1978

# Returning from the Beach

Sunset returns from the sandy beach
summer hides along the reef
In the ocean summer still whispers
its own name. I can't help reflecting on
the secret of seasonal change, time stopping
the truth and untruth of time
the wounds left by the cycle of ages. And I
hear the actors boisterously boarding the bus
some stand-ins cleaning up the props:
history does not allow tales of blood and tears to repeat
this moving play must come to an end
before dark. Once more I hear
a sunset bugle from the barracks
covering the sound of the distant fidgety surf

1978

## Evening Clouds

We lock evening clouds outside the low door
and watch a gray gull angle
over the wild strawberry field and head straight north
We observe the quiet breeze
unable to move a pink hibiscus . . . maybe
it's not a breeze: "If the hibiscus doesn't move
how can you tell there *is* a quiet breeze?"
"Sit tight. You be the hibiscus, I'll be the breeze"
She shakes her head coyly like pink twilight
listening to the promise of quiet brushing
across her fair arms and shoulders, her
collar and hair. Entering the dark
I see a firefly coming in from outside
stealthily, intentionally, it flits over her ankles

1978

# The First Snow

1.

The first snow of the winter
Surprise, some gentle
delight — now I can describe it
to satisfy your curiosity. Outside
the long windows of my office
like a cello accompanying a folksong, snow
watches me open and read the letter from far away
among piles of papers cluttering my desk
careful not to rip the two bright red
tropical tomatoes on the envelope

2.

This winter's first snow
seems to fall on brick walls and withered branches
I put your letter down — snow glare filling the room
shining on the tomato stamp
your name and address
You are fertile midsummer
living in dense, fresh greenness —
though you say a cold front just passed through
you still are, will always be

3.
The first snow of the winter
stops when night comes. In my office I'm typing
a paper about the methodology and mentality
of literary criticism
Tomorrow morning squirrels and young birds
will come out to type, too, on the snowy ground
a paper about walnuts, wings, and children's songs
I pick up an envelope
write down your name and address
Tomorrow I'll send you a photocopy

1978

# Hua-lien

The roaring surf outside the window is just
my age, born on the eve of the War
at the end of the Japanese occupation of Taiwan
Like me, he is a dragon
we share the same temperament and keep
some unimportant secrets for each other
Awake at midnight, I listen to him telling me of
what he's felt and thought since we parted

Some of his stories were too fantastic and trivial
so I didn't wake you up
I let you sleep, sleep peacefully
Tomorrow I'll pick the more interesting
and touching ones to tell you

Though like me he is a dragon, his heart is immense
his understanding deeper; he's even better than me at
controlling changing moods and thoughts
In the afternoon he surged quietly by the balcony
and watched you carefully
(you clung to me and smiled, thinking you were
looking at him when in fact he was looking at you)
because you are the fairest
the *most* fairest bride of my hometown

Now it's midnight, on such a deep night
with you sound asleep, he whispers beyond the railing
He says: "Come here, I have something
to tell you." I can't bear to
leave you in your sleep, so I turn around
and listen to his loving voice —
in the Mandarin we learned after the War

with a Taiwanese accent—speaking slowly, comfortingly
to a Hua-lien native who suddenly sheds tears

"Don't be sentimental," he says
"tears should fall for others not for yourself"
The waves thrash the rocky shore, autumn is always
like this, always. "You must be
as immense as I am, and understand more deeply:
The War didn't change us, so
you mustn't be discouraged by any setback"

Some of his words were too intense and serious
so I didn't wake you up
I let you sleep, sleep peacefully
Tomorrow I'll pick the more interesting
and moving ones to tell you

I want you to sleep, don't have the heart
to wake you up, even less to let you see me
cry from joy, from bringing you to my hometown
against the roaring surf on an autumn midnight
Tomorrow I'll reveal a small secret
to you: that's exactly what he says
he says you are the fairest
the *most* fairest bride of our hometown

1978

# Cicada

I wake up to the cicadas' transparent drone, contemplative, now that
a heated transparency covers last night's topic, sad but exciting,
covers it like a summer capsule for me to swallow, so I don't
frown when I chew.

I draw the curtains, searching. But how can this anxious drone guide
us? Besides the power of knowledge we also believe in the senses.
Yet, doesn't my frustration come from my resorting to the
senses, to the erroneous guidance of the senses?

They say a cicada's life is an apt symbol for the tragic hero. So humble
and slow, it persists and struggles. Once it leaves the moist soil,
it crawls up the tree trunk. I must praise its will to rise, its
lonely, brave will

taking shape in the rain and dew.

It passes knots on the tree trunk like circles in Dante's dream world;
it crawls along like pious faithful Dante, a Catholic pilgrim
trudging without hesitation toward the destined glorious world,
but glory is lonely.

Loneliness can't stay out of our super-sophisticated dialogue, one-
third classical skepticism and two-thirds Romantic passion. Last
night we discussed the future of our nation and society and the
pattern of history; we also tried to define love . . .

Love can't be defined. "For example," the other person analyzed, "to
be responsible only for one's passion and honesty, and still with
that passion and honesty hurt others. Short-lived obstinacy may
be more frightening than eternal indifference. Don't you think?"

I was speechless. The next day I woke up to the cicadas' transparent
drone, contemplating the sad but exciting issues of my nation

and society and history and the definition of love. I drew the
curtains, allowing the drone to guide me. I have found its
location. Once formed in the rain and dew,

it announces the end of life's journey with heated shrieking. I seem to
have found its glorious location, on the burning phoenix tree
directly before me, to the right.

1978

# In Memoriam: Albert Einstein

Last night you walked up to me kindly, in the legendary old sweater, in the shadows of newly blossoming magnolias. You couldn't help smiling as you asked me why I had not written a poem for you—Albert Einstein, great physicist, Jewish saint. "Besides," you said, "your office is next to mine. Have you never thought of me as you come and go?"

Great physicist, Jewish saint, Albert Einstein. They say your most stunning discovery, the theory of relativity, 1919, has something to do with the universe. I don't understand it, so it has nothing to do with me—but I, too, am a believer in relativity. Though I have heard about you, I don't know you.

In the shadows of newly blossoming magnolias, you urged me to write a poem for you. "Besides," you went on, "this year is my hundredth birthday. When you read in your office, have you never heard me move my chair or cough next door? In my old age, I no longer thought much about physics; most of the time I contemplated Jewish problems."

In contrast to your wrinkled forehead, sparse dogwoods outside the window wait for the warm spring to blossom. I stroll down the hallway, as if I heard your footsteps on the other side of the courtyard, but they can only be mine. No, you are strolling, thinking about Israel. I am thinking about Taiwan.

Science fascinates me. Exactly because I don't understand it, it fascinates me. I am sorry, Albert Einstein, you cannot move me, though Israel moves me. After the snow, I heard people talking about you everywhere. This town is famous because of you. When spring comes, they will still talk about you. Summer, fall, winter.

I am sorry I can't write a poem to commemorate you, I can't even talk
about you like everyone else, though many years ago I listened
enthusiastically to a Jew promoting Israel. As to the theory of
relativity, an earth-shaking event also took place in China, in
1919, and was known as the May Fourth Movement.

Albert Einstein, have you heard of the May Fourth Movement?
Mr. Democracy, Mr. Science: our blood and tears. Many have
died for democracy and science in China. Time to put sweet
grass everywhere, lighting up your words as I think of them:
*Raffiniert ist der Herrgott, aber boshaft ist er nicht.*

Your faith and wisdom are inscribed on the wall above the fireplace in
the lecture hall. I meditate in the magnolia shadows and sweet
grass light. I believe truth can be searched for, so can democracy
and science. The theory of relativity has nothing to do with me,
but I can be moved by Israel's struggle. Jewish saint, great
physicist, can you be moved by my Taiwan?

1979

# Conversation

This is all taking place at Princeton
The spring rain seems to have stopped
but drifts delicately. A light smoke
floats here and there over the treetops
I sit by the window waiting and looking
wondering how you are doing at school

A red-breasted bird on the lawn
looks for food as it jumps over clumps of green onions
It's quiet in the yard. By the window
I drink tea, smoke, read Ch'ü Yuan who crossed the river
I raise my head constantly to look out the window while you
drink coffee and practice English conversation at school

An old man walks his dog on the tennis court
The spring rain seems to have stopped; otherwise what will
you do after class without an umbrella?
It's enough for you to manage a little English conversation
I push away the book and look for your car—
as long as you come home safely everything's all right

1979

# Seven Turns of the Coast

On the seacoast where dark waves surge
we find a place for resting and living
(you have followed me in my prolonged wandering
with two rods, a sword and a spear)
On a slope overlooking a prairie and a valley with a stream
we find evergreen and fruit trees
a yard for you to practice martial arts, and a study

We are surprised to find that
on the seacoast where dark waves surge
life is brighter than sunlight, purer than
snow, braver than wind and thunder. The North
Star is witness to it all, everything
no matter which direction you observe from
standing tall, joyous, and strong

faster than the flapping wings of a seagull
flying over floating icebergs
by the seacoast where dark waves surge
searching for the legend of the heart, the legend of blood
the myth of green seaweed and coral—
under the palms of our hands, the vast
warm, bright ocean of life

Often I see curiosity
and anticipation fill the space between your eyes and brows
focusing on purity and energy
On the seacoast where dark waves surge
the giant whales' garden lies behind the heavy fog
ships at regular intervals detour around it as they
head straight for our homeland, Taiwan

When you tightly close your slender hands
they become two black belt fists
when open, now gently comb your short
pretty hair, or fold tiny baby clothes
on the seacoast where dark waves surge
As expected, a big ship proudly hoists anchor
and sails straight for our homeland, Taiwan

Everything looks simple and easy
all the preparing, cleaning, watering
of potted flowers, feeding of squirrels on the patio
crossing the road with a bamboo staff from Lu-ku village
and bringing back a bag full of mail
On the seacoast where dark waves surge
you open your brother's airmailed letter and newspapers

Now sunlight reaches farther
to fill your yard and my study
Spring will soon be here, our son
will live more fully, peacefully
in Taiwan; eloquent and strong
though he is born in another country
on the seacoast where dark waves surge

1980

# Annotations on Plants and Trees for Ying-ying
## (Selections)

*Bamboo*

Cleansed by the fresh shower, the spotted bamboo by the east fence
sways in immense light —
late autumn already in salmon's dreamland
Based on your accent and expressions
I imagine an expanse of summer ocean

Emerald and opulent like an ocean of warm
patient days, when the wind rises
it dances wildly like white waves
splashing onto a sandy beach of sunset clouds: a shining star
like a purple seashell beyond the bamboo

*White Birch*

Last night frost invaded it. When day breaks
fallen leaves drift onto the wet
steps by the side gate, little by little covering
the vegetable patch I worked so hard weeding
and the glistening snail trails on the slabs

The tree stands alone like an outdated
literary school casting its sound and shadow in the yard
I read about it in Sung dynasty lyrics and English poetry
identify it in Japanese tales. Sad and
morose, it is a page in literary history

*Beech*

Outside the window a woodblock print of tree rings
inside, the same. Fierce midsummer
sunset responds by teasing
the shadows of twigs and slender leaves, entangling
and overlapping their will to grow

I often imagine you taking a nap
in the lounge chair in serene autumn sunlight
and facing the precise form of the beech
Let the tree rings' revolving sound hush you in sleep
and guide your robust breathing and pulse

*Chinese Crabapple*
An old tree in the backyard drops golden fruit
reports the deepening of autumn—autumn is deep
Often you sit before the window and write a letter
a long letter, and suddenly hear
the thud of fruit falling to the ground like a period

Late autumn afternoon is filled with the sound of
ripe Chinese crabapples. You open the door, walk outside
and count how many have fallen to the lawn—
as many as the periods in your letter . . .
and drifting leaves the commas

*Rhododendron*
Each time I see it leaning against
the window of my study—most of the time quiet
with a shy expression. Originating in the south
of Cloud Ridge with its distant hills and streams
each flower tells a story of a kingdom's rise and fall

But how did it drift across the sea to lean in the light rain
against my window, shelves of T'ang and Sung romances beyond
to reveal in its shyness a surprise
and some destined love? Each flower hesitates
to speak, like a tearful poem without a title

*Juniper*
Spreading around the path near the front gate
like a silent, deep-thinking dragon—
slender hawthorn leaves fall on it

beech nuts, bird feathers, fallen petals . . .
"Flowered paths have not been swept to welcome guests' arrival"

After October, it looks more rickety
as if longing for the depth of the river
On cold nights I read Tu Fu under the lamp and hear
it sob through "Meditations on Autumn"
I imagine how lonely and dejected it must be

1980

# Fourteen Sonnets for Ming-ming (Selections)

I.

After wind and rain, bright
sunlight wakes up clover, lichen, and ferns
Leaning on each other we cross the lawn to examine
the damp wall that exudes the smell of early spring.
In the northwest corner we plant
a Chinese ilex and fix the side gate
with nails. A whole night of wind and rain follows
On our life's giant ancient zither
the taut strings of prophecy open up an expanse
of solemnity and grandeur. In opulent March
we lean on each other in the early morning chill
wait in anticipation, listen to the farthest
rain clouds gradually gather and disperse at sea:
a glorious horn, a precise point on the drum

2.

On that perfect day, we
witness winter chill gradually yielding to spring warmth
On both sides of the long bridge, a sonic boom
at daybreak makes the vast misty lake splash
Life chose that day
with superb determination and thundering strength
that perfect day to proclaim to us . . .
After sunrise a fine snow
at noon a shower cleanses the sober earth
Mountain ranges rise higher, rivers flow faster
blue pines clamor and hurry in the wind. In an instant
a flock of white birds flits over the sprouting
prairie, flying hail knocks on the sea-facing window
You have chosen a perfect day to arrive

5.

This is your kingdom, domain of milk
your first home like a strawberry island
on a thousand miles of windy waves. Remember, the blue expanse
beyond a thousand miles of windy waves is our home
Be like that, but a million times more immense and grand
Remember the subtropical south of bananas and pineapples
the west coast of blue sky and vast sea, the fair peaks
of a volcano chain thrusting through the snow line
All the rivers run in the four directions and look
to the ocean in anticipation. This is
your kingdom, the encampment where we assemble
in the rainy northern moderate zone
I want you to know the latitude and longitude of this yard:
strawberry and milk. You begin from here

8.

Beyond seventh heaven, at the beginning
and end of the universe, the sea of stars glitters forever
and we identify with it. So familiar
your voice and face, so familiar
A long long time ago, in another
time and age, we were one—
form and shadow traveled side by side
beyond a seventh heaven of incomparable silence
resisted, with a will beyond memory
arrogant human law and philosophy
challenged rage's authority with indifference
with an inexplicable, inimitable smile
Once we trudged across mountains and rivers side by side
in search of justice, righteousness, and compassion in the human world

11.

The wind blows down the valley too, the river originates
from primitive tranquility. Tattoos, humming cicadas—

this is our secret world, filled with
the unreachable, and it cannot be portrayed
with your limited crayons. A body-burning heat
comes from the other end of childhood; once frustrated and cooled
in my lifetime, it leads to this end of childhood, burning as before
No need for you to be afraid. Walk toward the blooming
betel palms, use simple dialect
and polite, friendly gestures that suit
the occasion, return people's curiosity with smiles—
they will support you like a brother of the tribe
at home, in our inviolable land

13.

You will like the sounds of our homeland
listen closely to the temple bell
the drum, the breeze brushing over sugarcane fields
carrying ancient, sweet beliefs. Yes
once people were lost in discussion and debate
lost in rumor and fury
We have found a solid vantage point
from which to observe scampering, insidious dust—
flippant, ridiculous manifestoes and accusations—because
we too were once lost, but after serious
contemplation have chosen the stature of blue mountains
and the coolness and vigor of springs. We
entered the city from the country, now we have
returned, clean and energized like a new drum

14.

This is the beginning, in the sound of the horn
a day of bells and drums. Gentle wind and rain
abundant sunlight form your bedspread, and spring
daffodils and bees have filled the
domain of your speedy growth. Waving your
powerful arms, you decorate the sky with brilliant

musical notes. You must get to know them
so you may rule them. Let wild geese in ranks
be the western longitude, splashing whales be the northern latitude
moonlight colored with peace, twinkling stars
adorn the bed where you learn to lift your head and turn over
Carriages and ships wait at the post
precise like a symphony, the seal versus the scribe style of calligraphy
a sartorial pattern in classical symmetry, a sonnet sequence

1980

# Midautumn Night

Returning to the small window, we guard
the new moon. Serene lake, snowy mountain
a jug of lukewarm wine
a few delicate thoughts
in the fresh-brewed cool air of a different country
The moon moves slowly around the mast of a silent ship
moored in the harbor

Know the moon you invite in
when you raise the curtain, a celestial rabbit
peeping at a sleeping reef. Waves surge
between our touches, wind and clouds churning
A soldier at a distant frontier
climbs the fortress
nostalgia his handhold

A dog barks downhill
wild grass like snow, dazzling brightness
in the woods. I look again—
the moon has crossed over the belltower

1980

# Midautumn

In morning chill I open the door and look around. A yellow sparrow
flutters low through the garden's white fog
Grass quivers then stops, shaking off a few dewdrops
This deep, mature quietude
buries an ancient tune. Tonight the moon
will rise over distant reeds

A bit intoxicated, I recite a melancholy
English sonnet in silence
peaceful, but somewhat blocked
my steps hesitate. Apples drop to the ground
knocking out an ancient tune. Tonight the moon
will rise over the distant river delta

I bend down to look at shy yellow chrysanthemums in bud
The little garden complains about the invasion of last night's frost—
with simple rhetoric, precise metaphors
it presents a powerful argument by the fence, unwittingly
composing an ancient tune. Tonight the moon
will rise over a distant balcony

1980

## Playing in Puddles after Rain

Often I get to know the shapes of flowing water
in wisteria shadows and see pincushions and rocking horses
in folded book pages. A distant city where
someone is taking a walk before her bath, crossing the street
with the speed of a star. A basket of flowers in her left hand, a child in
        her right
she stops in front of a bakery and bends down
to tie the child's shoelaces. The setting sun recedes from the treetops
looks back hesitantly and vanishes from the seashore
in late T'ang dynasty poses

Or, before dusk covers the hill
everything is at rest: lying on the grass
I watch the wind brush hibiscus flowers and reminisce . . .
Snails crawl slowly on the wooden wall
pigeons fly over the jungle of antennas on the rooftops
Three streets away a car slams on its brakes—
then a moment of peace. But in that peace
I hear

tiny red shoes ambling through a yard
of clover in dew-moist morning light
in search of a hibiscus flower or a snail
trail from yesterday . . . Then all things of the past fade
without my awareness. When she combs her hair under a night-light
her eyes still speak of spring: glittering lights in the air
shine on a pond of slender waterlilies. I often combine
metaphysical details at will—a hat, a skirt
a parasol—in sketching a child born of sunlight
how she sleeps quietly in pear blossom scent

In wisteria shadows
her curly reddish-black hair on a pillow
her temperament as pliant as clouds trailing a dragon
as stormy as a gust accompanying a tiger—surging and clutching
in my memory, gnawing my trembling
worrying heart. I wonder whether it's the Southern Cross
or the Big Dipper; a shadow snoops
outside the curtained window and peeps at the child's slender brows
long eyelashes, and rounded nose. Corners of her lips are calm
as a bay in moonlight
her seashell ears listen to
the wind and its conversation with the sea

Her shoulders lean on a dream naturally
a handsome hill
moving up and down abstractly. Every minute she grows
her tiny limbs stretch and flow into my book stacks
my notes, annotations, proofs, bibliographies, and translations—
the contrast between images and rhymes resembles a dragon in the clouds
a tiger commanding the wind, like lips and teeth
like breasts and heart, like sister and brother
playing in puddles after the rain

Someone feeds the waterbirds by the willows, then she stops
to straighten the white hat on her child's head


1981

# Rapids

**1.**

Rapids in the woods, clouds over a whirlpool
I turn around by the water's edge and look through short
reeds—you sitting by the window in the log cabin
I think this is the dawn of the universe
stars recede one by one
returning the immense desolation
to time
fish reproduce in the upper stream, hibernating bears
sleep through last year's wounds
on the other shore a puff of smoke rises
as peaceful as a flute

I lay my cap on the stone step
my hair gray in dew
I sit and wait for wild geese to fly over the stream, listen to drums
sink slowly to the wooden bridge on the other shore
sunrays like arrows

**2.**

This is the twilight of the earth; with complex eyes time watches
the multifarious secrets of the rapids—
countless knots tied and untied, untied then tied again—
swirling, relaxing under the coniferous forest
and flowing to the sea. Like yesterday—
the autumn of another age—
insects shriek on the bank, moss
on the steps darker than volition
the color of fire in the fireplace swift like wine

You skim through an art book found
in the hallway, I proofread a collection

of critical essays from my early days
About to fall, chrysanthemums on the coffee table
are held up by the sunset
Your eyes turn to the hallway:
fishing pole, galoshes, raincoat, cap—

they play noisily in the rapids
circulating splashes, wavy episodes
sometimes they look at each other in silence, searching
for each other's eyes: how can my sluggishness
kindle your desire to keep us warm?
They know each other's gills
and the fire's color as swift as wine
exaggerated like the hand's gesture for love
a singer's hair hanging loose
a dancer's outfit

3.
It is the age when wars have stopped
we travel through the woods in heavy fog, walk up
to the deserted water's edge, turn around
no longer able to find the footprints
of a previous life. We build a fire in silence
read some unimportant books
rapids in the woods
clouds above a whirlpool

1981

# Incomplete Trio

I sit in the lobby, tired
watching human shadows and cars changing colors on a returning
autumn afternoon. Fallen leaves are blown up by low sounds
drifting across the street, falling slowly back on the street's wet slabs
Sitting under an exaggerated chandelier, I imagine
some past moment, or maybe the next moment—
when fallen leaves are blown high by autumn wind and fall again—
suddenly she pushes the door open, enters, overlapping faces and voices
transcending time, hurries to the sagging sofa where I sit
raises her eyebrows, smiles at me, and with her hands pulls me up
from my tired seat. Her smile carries some surprise and fear, her
    ice-cold fingers
clutch my left hand while her breasts lean on my right arm
as if pleading for love, sympathy, and understanding

I am pleading, too:
Let us go back to the primeval wilderness of newborn ferns (or maybe
a little later), back to the age of echoing prairies
thirty-five millennia after the glaciers. Conversing wildflowers
like multicolored birds, springs look for paths
for life's riverbed and often change directions
lively and vigorous like robust sperm swimming in song
changing personality and posture at different temperatures
in different soils: sometimes deep in earth, turning like a hidden whirlpool
sometimes flowing on the surface over reedy sandhills, slowing into a
    swamp
An infinite message waits for sunlight to disclose and spread
to be analyzed by thunder and lightning, interpreted by wind and rain
The space is too immense to start; flowers in conversation
birds practice eugenics

By then darkness has withdrawn
In our oversight, even civilization begins to
decline. Possession is the only moderation and sympathy that exists . . .
A low bell chime comes from love's temple
shaking off the lingering snow of medieval times, torrents
cut open the black forest, riders gallop
along the water's edge—with a solemn, secret mission
to advocate an idea and overthrow the last dynasty
Their hooves swift, a little irregular too
like a morning breeze flapping hypocritical banners, tearing apart
tightly strung desire and pride, sharp scissors cutting through fabric
leaving a deep scar of moderation and sympathy

A cup of wine is passed around. In another age
blood and tears stop, the age of spears and halberds, bows and arrows
Some people grope in the night after sacrificial rituals
testing one another's pulse, delighted and consoled
Peaceful looks fall into the cup, revealing
a covenant with angels, their vast, soundless wings
flapping solemnly in the still dusk, waiting for night to fall
After sacrificial rituals, they grope and test
identify one another's arms and body. But
in midnight's skin color, there is a song
soft as moonlight, like embroidery, waterlily scent
like hair warmer than wine on echoing prairies
tightened straw sandals lost in immense space
Flowers in conversation, birds practice eugenics
as if pleading for love, sympathy, and understanding
I am pleading, too

I sit in the lobby, tired
watching human shadows and cars changing colors outside the door
        on a returning
autumn afternoon. Fallen leaves are blown up by low sounds

drifting across the street, falling slowly back on the street's wet slabs
Sitting under an exaggerated chandelier, I imagine
some past moment, or maybe the next moment—

1981

# Flying Through the Human World

It happened on a cold afternoon, as if in
another time and age, another universe beyond the nebulas
A dark and dense coniferous forest still insisted on its ancient face
born of the breath of sea and high wind. Once I was lost—
flying slowly, searching, between a meteor and an abandoned spaceship
like a UFO, oblivious to time
and forgotten by time. But when the temperature dropped suddenly
at the edge of the Sea of Tranquillity, my shadow
brushed past another strange landscape—in that instant
I recalled a coniferous forest dark and dense like an ancient memory
     sinking
into the warmth of morning light. Following a cold current
I lost speed and was propelled into another time and age

        The winter sun brightens the mountain slope shyly
        sieving through giant withered trees . . .
        Sparrows sprinkling the parking lot
        are startled by my footsteps, take off and
        gather at a distant spot. Around the railing
        I walk to higher ground and look around
        the winter sun warming my back
        casting my long shadow
        stretching toward lingering snow
        On the chair to my left a decrepit Indian sits quietly

According to the frequencies of human concern, my speed changed
     constantly
I stopped in the center of a desert, speculating about
the origin and end of life, blood like a surging river
flowing into receptive lakes, forming a few uneasy
whirlpools. I looked back, the path I came on is beyond thought

Maybe it took place in the middle of the farthest, oldest town
inconceivable like a face you see in a dream
a quivering cry, pain touched with joy, the color of the hair
changing with its length, shining through the window blinds

        Flocking ducks scramble for food
        in the heart of a frozen lake; they slip and fall
        into the water, then with difficulty waddle back
        onto the ice flapping their wings. The winter sun brightens
        the children's laughter as they play
        loudly: throwing bread crumbs far far
        into the heart of the lake, watching ducks
        scramble for them, slipping into the water and
        waddling back to the ice, proudly flapping their wings

It was probably summer in a small subtropical town, in ancient times
when phoenix trees were not yet completely extinct
Once in a cabin where cold air flew by, we embraced to keep each
      other warm
chewed on metallic clatter glittering in memory, vivid
forceful, and precise, more delightful than heartbeats
Now that I look back, the path I came on was buried deep
in the dust of time. But I can still vaguely see
beyond antiquity, when cicada drone and golden sun changed by turn
when I was determined to travel far and, ready to go, blasted off
I chose a route that no one else was willing to try, a lonely voyage
I destroyed the secret transmission code of the universe, abandoned time
and somehow was abandoned by time in the ensuing emptiness

        The Indian man stumbles up
        takes a squint at the icy lake, and walks off
        A purple bamboo shivers in the wind
        the children are running. Someone
        throws a piece of ice from the other shore
        clanking like the quick strings of an ancient zither

Astounded, they stand around
and watch the broken ice splashing and flying
its echoes rising in suspension
and congealing in the grove
Shyly an early rising moon
brightens their amused eyes and brows

I look back at the path I came on, recalling
the words and gestures before I left: How did life begin?
In remote antiquity, when pledges were pure and bright
in a corner of the earth like naked bodies curving and relaxing
secrets like fireflies drifting across the tips of the hair, hard like
    clashing pelvic bones
transcending abstraction and returning to reality. Life was frail tadpoles
struggling in shallow water; not having enough time to grow into
    croaking frogs
they bore even smaller tadpoles in silence. In antiquity
when evolution took too much wisdom, patience
and courage, we couldn't wait: we broke the abstract law of inheritance
transcended nature's restrictions, God's decree, and morality
and entered directly into the essence of love and desire . . .

I bend over the bone-piercing
lake water with the winter sun behind me
and the moon before me seeming to overlap
spreading the chill. I pick up
a brick of ice and throw it hard
toward the other shore. With a thud the ice breaks
in the heart of the lake, spreading around like
the very beginning when the universe
exploded for the first time into zillions of
misty shapes. It sounds like a phoenix crying, like planets
    clashing
crumbling, coming together, falling apart

A familiar sound, like
the beginning when I first set out on
the lonely voyage, what I saw and heard
in another time and age, oblivious to time
and forgotten by time
losing speed and direction
a courageous UFO

1982

# Crows Crying in the Night

*The moon bright, trees without leaves,*
*Frost slippery, wind between branches.*

Po Chü-yi (772–846)

A shower subsides in the evening wind
concealing riverside trees
on the river's far bank in
misty clouds, but the gleaming sunset
gradually unfolds in my
long gaze like
the sound of an ancient musical instrument

"Only love and politics
can save your soul"
Its origin is far far away
like an exotic lute drifting by accident across
the prairie of a former dynasty, a horn
tumbling and returning from a distant land
a mature compassion
smooth and full, a ripping sound
mixed with anxiety and uneasiness
so intense it breaks at last with a clang
the main string's high note
shatters the sobbing pipe

Restraint, perseverance, insistence
history like
the ripened
fruit
of that autumn
containing infinite
compassion and sympathy

When the setting sun shines on the valley
"Only love and politics can
save your soul"
too dazzling to gaze
serene like a running spring
in silence
I anticipate a storm and mudslide
When stars go out one by one
I listen in the dark
to high waves and
the howls of wolves

The next life is uncertain
this life has just begun
The morning rain cleanses the earth
"Only love and politics can save
your soul." I murmur:
"Confirm
my body"


1982

# Mount Rainier, 1983

*Ch'ü Yuan's poems are actually allegories;*
*Followers try to mimic him in vain.*

Fan Ch'eng-ta (1126–93)

*Buddhist Nun*
Between early winter and midwinter
an expanse of startled sunset
pine needles and dry leaves gently
skim the mist by the water
In the distance, on the boundary between being and nonbeing
a flock of birds flies by
maybe lingering wild geese
heading south before they migrate north
disappearing into cold air, returning from the mist
to the void

Solemn and peaceful like the beginning of the cosmos
a mountain sitting still, calming
the minds of crying gibbons and the hearts
of galloping horses—she conquers
sorrow and joy with indifference
illuminates love with lovelessness

*Shamaness*
A hill lying sideways, her trailing gown
cascades from the couch. Too high to see
her face buried deep in the clouds
but judging from the folds of her skirt
she is smiling

She had just completed
an elaborate ritual

after prayers and incense, she stood
to offer flowers, then prostrated herself
sashes and sleeves in disarray
Piously she communed with the sea
the sun, the moon, stars, and constellations
ice, snow, clouds, and rain
wind

*Queen*
The mountain still lies there, her opulent body
covered with velvet
I imagine the way her feet cross each other
as blood flows downward from the heart. She dreams
frowns happily in her sleep, contented

Worries? None. But
even in the tired bed
she maintains a style
of feminine virtue—
saintly, proper, occasionally trivial
Her ornate hair is too high to see
and when she breathes peacefully
the purest jade under heaven
quivers and shakes rhythmically
at the end of a sash across her stomach

*Courtesan*
The mountain bows and nods. Before her knees
a lustrous old zither
waiting nonchalantly
for wine cups to be put down, human noises
to stop, frogs and insects of the grass to hold their breath
As to the wind? The wind rests on the autumn moon roof

Her melodic fate
flows from the seven strings as she

opens her mouth and sings: "The one I miss is
in the Rockies. I would follow him but yellow sands
keep us apart. I turn east to gaze, rain wets my clothes
The Fair One gave me a pepper flower
I reciprocate with an ash-handled sword
The way is too far to travel; I wander. Why do I worry
why is my heart troubled? The one I miss is
in the Congo. I would follow him but the road is treacherous
I turn south to gaze and listen to the wind
The Fair One gave me glistening tears
I reciprocate with shining agate. The way is too far
to travel; I am disconsolate. Why do I worry
why is my heart sad? The one I miss
is in Yi-lan. I would follow him but the sea is cold
I turn west to gaze at misty clouds. The Fair One
gave me a jeweled sword; I reciprocate with a precious dagger
The way is too far to travel; I linger. Why do I worry
why does my heart fret? The one I miss
is in remote darkness. I would follow him but the snow never stops
I turn north to gaze and listen in silence
The Fair One gave me a fishing pole; I reciprocate with a phoenix mirror
The way is too far to travel; I sigh
Why do I worry, why is my heart disturbed?"

The mountain bows and nods
the wind rests on the autumn moon roof

*Doctor of Philosophy*
Sometimes she is slender and solemn
A gauze hat, a delicate hair knot
her eyelashes lowered for a long while, then startled
they flutter up and down —
sharp as a bee's kiss, a sweet look
in the eye. The mountain is a learned woman
a copy editor

The moon rises
She reads under a solitary lamp
her feet on a cozy
cushion, hidden under the long dress
her heels nestled against the calves. Her heart beats
as she interprets the eloquent rhetoric of classical sophists
imagines the charm of ancient scholars
gesturing elegantly. "If the dead could be revived"
she sighs: "whom would I choose?"

*Swordswoman*
The mountain wears a pale blue cape
Gazing far off, the austere
look reminds me of a swordsman about to travel a thousand miles
to rescue those in trouble
Long hair on the shoulder—yes, it is
a swordswoman

Willow leaf brows and phoenix eyes, a film of frost
on her face (I wonder what causes her
to look so austere)
A gust of wind shakes the candle flame on the table
it flickers. She pulls the long sword
from the scabbard and examines it, a cold glint on her face
She remembers a tangled romance from the past—
the white stallion, west wind, boat dock
by chance she turned her face to a jade flute tune . . .
A red cloud drifts across her determined
cheeks, now lost and tender

*Immortal*
She is that kind of reticent, enchanting Taoist nun
A rosy twilight cloud
twirls and shines in a midsummer evening
It symbolizes an ancient discipline

of asceticism and purity, her transcendent
abstinent body devoid of
calories and fat

The lake murmurs
She lifts her face and looks around, reciting
the mumbo jumbo of tigers and leopards and
the virgin's heart spells. A hydrofoil
glides over the waves, breaks
the reflection of her gaze. After all, she
is one of that enchanting kind

1983

# Tree in the College

At the end of a long corridor, in the warm, quiet
slanting winter sunlight, through half-open windows
pours an expanse of curved, fierce green
I bend forward to look at the tree closely, with a shape
between violence and sympathy
an ever-growing metaphor
Like an unbending hero arming himself, the shady leaves in sharp pain
cover a lawn of idylls and lyrics
I concentrate and see thousands of golden phoenix eyes
gazing up at fish-shaped clouds floating across the sky
Like a sailor in the Age of Great Voyages
on a long, disciplined quest
I look at the calm humid sea south of the Tropic of Cancer
north of the Tropic of Cancer
to find, unexpected, a seasonal aquatic tribe
swimming silently to the west

> "A butterfly," a little girl exclaims
> I turn around to see her—
> she must be a professor's daughter—
> staring enviously at a half-open window:
> "I want that colorful butterfly . . ."
> We approach the resting pansy whose
> wings close in a dream. "I want to
> catch it, then I'll put it in a book. It won't hurt"

It won't hurt, but it will die
and leave behind a dry, colorful dress without a soul
in the embrace of a book, close to words
not necessarily living in the sympathy and wisdom that
we seek. I lower my head to look at the little girl

with faint dark hair and pale brows. Someday
she will grow up with books, lean on the window
notice and marvel at a tree that rises high in the air
It will surprise her with its gestures of sympathy
and wisdom, its phoenix eyes—now kind with age—still gazing at the
    clouds
swinging like banners or butterflies in spring breeze
"I'll be an old man then," I say
"but I will always remember you"

    She smiles gleefully toward a half-open
    window: "Would you like to see
    soap bubbles?"

At the end of a long corridor, in the warm, quiet
slanting winter sunlight, the little girl scoops up a string of colorful
    bubbles
and blows them toward nothingness. A pale shadow fades into
the courtyard of savage green, like winking beautiful eyes
missing the flickering sunlight
vanishing in the wind
With hands on the rail I look out
Strings of bubbles drift by
the tree sheds leaves solemnly
By then we'll both be old—
without our dry, colorful clothes, we will have only an awakened soul
in the embrace of a book, close to words
living in the sympathy and wisdom that we seek

1983

# Someone Asks Me about Justice and Righteousness

Someone asks me about justice and righteousness
in a neatly written letter
mailed from a town in another county, signed
with his real name, including social security number
age (outside my window rain drips on banana leaves
and broken glass on garden walls), ancestry, occupation
(twigs and branches pile up in the yard
a black bird flaps its wings). Obviously he has
thought long without reaching an answer to this important
question. He is good at conceptualization, his
writing is concise, forceful, and well-organized
his penmanship presentable (dark clouds drift toward the far end
     of the sky) —
he must've studied calligraphy in the Mysterious Tower style. In
     elementary school, he
probably lived in congested public housing in a back alley behind a
     fishing harbor
He spent most of his time with his mother, he was shy and
self-conscious about speaking Mandarin with a Taiwanese accent
He often climbed the hill to watch the boats at sea
and white clouds — that's how his skin got so dark
In his frail chest a small
solitary heart was growing — he writes frankly
"precocious as a Twentieth Century pear"

Someone asks me about justice and righteousness
With a pot of tea before me, I try to figure out
how to refute with abstract concepts the concrete
evidence he cites. Maybe I should negate his premise first
attack his frame of mind and criticize his fallacious way of
gathering data, in order to weaken his argument

Then point out that all he says is nothing but bias
unworthy of a learned man's rebuttal. I hear
the rain getting heavier and heavier
as it pours down the roof and fills gutters
around the house. But what is a Twentieth Century pear?
They were found in the island's mountainous region
a climate comparable to the northern China plains
and transplanted to the fertile, abundant virgin land
a seed of homesickness that sprouted, grew
and bore flowers and fruit—a fruit
whose pitiful shape, color, and smell were not mentioned in classics
Other than vitamin C its nutrient value is uncertain
It symbolizes hardly anything
but its own hesitant heart

Someone asks me about justice and righteousness
They don't need symbols—if it is reality
then treat it as such
The writer of the letter has an analytical mind
After a year in business management, he transferred to law. After
        graduation
he served in the army reserve for six months, took the bar exams twice . . .
The rain has stopped
I cannot comprehend his background, or his anger
his reproach and accusations
though I have tried, with the pot of tea
before me. I know he's not angry at the exams, because they aren't among his
        examples
He speaks of issues at a higher level, in a precise, forceful
well-organized manner, summarized in a sequence of confusing
questions. The sun trickles onto the lawn from behind the banana trees
glitters among old branches. This isn't
fiction—an immense, cold atmosphere persists
in this scant warmth

Someone asks me a question about
justice and righteousness. He was the neatest in his class
though his mother was a laundry woman in town. In his memory
the fair-skinned mother always smiled even when tears
streamed down her face. With her soft, clean hands
she sharpened pencils for him under a lamp
Can't remember clearly, but it was probably on a muggy night
after a fiery quarrel his father—his impassioned speech and heavy
        accent that even his
only son could not fully understand—
he left home. Maybe he went up to the mountains
where the climate resembles the North China plains to cultivate
a newly transplanted fruit, the Twentieth Century pear
On autumn nights his mother taught him Japanese nursery rhymes
about Peach Boy's conquest of Devil Island. With sleepy eyes he
watched her rip out the seams of old army uniforms
and scissor them into a pair of wool pants and a quilted jacket
Two water marks on the letter, probably his tears
like moldy spots left by the rain in the corner. I look outside
Earth and heaven have cried, too, for an important question
that transcends seasons and directions. They have cried
then covered their embarrassment with false sunlight

Someone asks me a question about
justice and righteousness. An eerie spider
hangs upside down from the eaves, bobs in the false
sunlight and weaves a web. For a long while
I watch winter mosquitoes fly in a dark cloud
around a plastic pail by the screen door
I have not heard such a lucid and succinct
argument in a long time. He is merciless in analyzing himself
"My lineage has taught me that wherever I go I will always
carry homesickness like a birthmark
But birthmarks come from the mother, and I must say mine

has nothing to do with it." He often

stands on the seashore and gazes far away. He's told that where mists and
    waves end

there is an even longer coastline, beyond them, mountains, forests, and vast rivers

"The place that Mother has never seen is our homeland"

In college, he was required to study modern Chinese history, and he
    memorized the book.

from cover to cover. He took linguistic sociology

did well in labor law, criminology, history of law but

failed physical education and the constitution. He excels in citing evidence

knows how to infer and deduce. I have never

received a letter so full of experience and fantasy

fervor and despair with a cold, poignant voice

a letter that strikes a perfect balance between fervor and despair

asking me, politely, about justice and righteousness

Someone asks me a question about justice and righteousness

in a letter that permits no addition or deletion

I see the tear marks expanding like dried-up lakes

In a dim corner fish die after failing to save each other

leaving white bones behind. I also see

blood splashing in his growing knowledge and judgment

like a pigeon released from a besieged fortress under fire—

a faint hope of the exhausted yet persevering resistance—

it breaks away from the suffocating sulfur smoke

soars to the top of a stench-filled willow tree

turns around swiftly and darts toward the base of reinforcement troops

but on its way is hit by a stray bullet

and crushed in the deafening encounter, its feathers, bones, and blood

fill a space that will never exist

and is quickly forgotten. I feel

in his hoarse voice that he once

walked in a wasteland, crying out

and screaming at a storm

Counting footsteps, he is not a prophet
He is no prophet but a disciple who has lost his guide
In his frail chest that pumps like a furnace
a heart melts at high heat
transparent, flowing, empty

1984

# Journey

*I long to cross the sky but have no feathered wings.*
                                                    Meng Chiao (751–814)


It is the coolest morning of summer
Before the sun rises to that corner
looks down and warms her curtains
the neighbor's cat tiptoes across
the yard of clover, jumps on the picnic table
turns around and looks in—smudging dewy flower color—
sees her pack a suitcase
with some light clothes, binoculars, a few books

She puts her handbag on the suitcase, then sits
at the foot of her bed, lost in thought about something
or some things. Inside the house
human shadows shift as in an intergalactic star war
you can even hear echoes of surf between the four walls
beating on the love-filled space inch by inch—
a gusty wind blows through a howling forest
rolling off the field of wild mushrooms, swarming to the dark
valley, awakening beasts and birds
sending them scampering and hovering without direction

All ends abruptly. She stands up and walks quickly
to the window. On the picnic table the neighbor's cat
stretches in bright sunlight, arches
and relaxes its holy, tranquil essence
She smiles at the coolness, turns around and looks in the mirror
winking at the crimson lips on a curious face
She picks up the suitcase, the bag with a bronze bell on her shoulder
exits the door, pulls it to and locks it
She walks to the mouth of the alley to wait for the bus. Cool and
        shady . . .
In the distant world all is warm and bright


1984

# Panjshir Valley

*In memory of an Afghani friend, who once said to me:*
*"Panjshir Valley is beautiful like Chinese women's eyes."*

In Panjshir Valley
when spring retreats with my people, we know
the enemies assemble on the steppe like pouring rain
We know because we once ran
through muddy prairies and streets wearing
wet cotton clothes and hats: spring
belonged to us, so did summer
Time in Panjshir Valley belonged
to us. In Panjshir Valley when spring
leaves temporarily, plants and trees grow better than last year
maybe nourished by gunsmoke and
toxic gas, maybe because of the war —
I can still hear the shuffling feet of my people
the constant bursts of gunfire, the ambushes
at noon and dusk and dawn

In Panjshir Valley they set up the
headquarters of occupation troops with countless posts
The Red Army in clusters patrols the villages
my people watch in silence
as they saw wood, shell peas
draw water from the well; in the warm damp air
a baby's cry suddenly rises
My people work in humiliation
live in sobs. They have no tears
In dry Panjshir Valley
a few vultures circle

snakes swish between boulders and gravel, scorpions
and lizards suck the last drop of blood from the dead

Often my people lie waiting on the narrow path
leading from Panjshir Valley to Andebula
In dense night air they grope toward enemy
camps, keeping close to home where they used to herd sheep
firing rockets, attacking
the invader's truck fleets; usually before
daybreak, bombings tear the deep-sleeping earth apart
Running through dry groves and over hills
they have no unit numbers
The helicopter rotors come closer and closer
machine guns sweep the prairie where we used to herd sheep
like a shower sweeping across dreams, but
spring will belong to us, summer will belong to
us, too, when plants and trees flourish more each day
the sheep will grow with our children
whose crying will fill a Panjshir Valley
that belongs to us, belongs completely to us

1984

# Wolves

I.

I hear the sound of my approaching kin
like a wind from the deepest trench in a distant sea
crystals of affection lodged in reef coral
jarred by a volcano's revival and
disturbed by schools of colorful fish—in a flash
waves fly by like dark hair, sweep through my days
like deftly plucked strings—
bring slaughter and tenderness that
blind me
as if I'd stared a burning meteor
into the dark Eastern Sea
When a wind rises—
suddenly awakens, then explodes—

I grope to hear
their flickering sound
It is the light of the universe, time and space
clashing against the cliff's icy forehead. Like a hunter
who can't lose his way, I am terrified
In the silence of a frozen lake
I hear the simple pulse of
my long-absent kin
quietly telling me of violence and beauty, and aspirations
like a wind from a distant sea, like crystals crumbling
The stormy surge leaves me blind but aware
that on the frozen lake, under the golden sun
stands a gentle, magnificent
snow-white wolf

2.

Under bright light
I see ants crawl
across a riverbed's dryness, rush
in indecipherable directions
Maybe they image our previous lives:
hardened warriors engage, shout
in the wilderness, insist on imprecise beliefs
they march to a drum beat, clash and die
They image our previous lives, petty ants
under the scrutiny of bright light
Standing before a giant locust tree, I am
the uneasiest believer in a skeptical age

I hear the sound of my approaching kin
in a strange tune like jade jingling against skin
a melody with a pendulum sway between two extremes
Then I'm aware the rushing ants could not
image our previous lives. They
crawl up from the dry riverbed
around my wet feet
and into the locust tree. Amid ritual bells and cannons
the few seats are assigned with solemnity
as I hear the sound of my approaching kin
like a forest that grows on a distant mountain
like reeds spreading over a boundless swamp
like the green moss that buries palaces—
and they are us
I turn to ask you something, in the spring breeze I see
a gentle, magnificent
snow-white wolf

3.

That day I walked by
the ancient temple seen in prophecy

In its still I heard the sound of my kin
approaching from some unknown quarter
The sun set over the ruins
cicada songs crowded sultry foothills
bees swirled in the gardenias
flies lit on dragon-embossed pillars
I glanced around before entering
the pine grove in search of the sound's origin
Looking into the stagnant water of an old well
I saw miasmic fog gather in the deadly heat
Could this be the prophesied resting place
on my long journey?
The Buddha smiled, arhats held their breath
ogres bowed down and stared
at silent incense burners

At the foot of the distant mountain—
as if it were the mundane world
no longer of my concern—
clamorous things are happening
as if they mattered
to me. Cicadas drone close to my ear
bees work among gardenias
Startled from sleep, birds in the plantain grove
beat their wings and stray into the Buddha's holy temple
I sit wordless, contemplating swift changes
and see in the tree's vacant, mottled shadow
a gentle, magnificent
snow-white wolf

4.
Autumn is deep
Troubled by the austerity of the air
we hold hands without speaking, cultivate melancholy
A few pots of yellow flowers in the patio, leaves piled high

on the balcony, my book cast aside by the fireplace
I push the back door open and catch sight of
a flock of wild geese
at the end of the sky

Autumn is deep
Autumn is a counterfeit heart
I hear the sound of my kin
approaching from an unidentifiable direction of the wild
so strange and so familiar it shakes
our chilled hearts as it flits across the shallow brook
the sheaf of dry wheat, sparrows' nests, cowsheds, snakes' sloughed skins
and ripe fruit in baskets
A gentle sound, with a will to
slaughter, following Time's golden cyclical rule
it savagely, lovingly lays siege to my heart—
cuts me with dancing reeds
holds me with the fullness of a pear, then teases me
with bunches of rhododendron buds
All that is true. I've heard
this season is a counterfeit heart. But

autumn is deep
Listless and tired, I lift my head above my writing
I rise in the cold air
to close the back door and retrieve the book by the fireplace
but everywhere between words and lines I see
a gentle, magnificent
snow-white wolf

1984

# Looking Down (Li-wu Stream, 1983)

> *For I have learned*
> *To look on nature, not as in the hour*
> *Of thoughtless youth, but hearing oftentimes*
> *The still, sad music of humanity,*
> *Nor harsh nor grating, though of ample power*
> *To chasten and subdue . . .*
>
> William Wordsworth

Suppose this time we use your perspective as the vantage point
The profound mirage of a supreme void reflects light from a thousand
    feet below
calling my name gently. Looking up
surely you see me bending
a survivor, my forehead perspiring a little
from being touched, my arms insisting on balance and
reason. Yes, you know me
like trees and grass up here
after wind and rain, frost and snow, my hair—
yet unlike trees and grass moving from flourish to decay
and then to reborn perfection—
my temples are mottled, but not as gray as when we parted
in a previous life. You know me
my stern face covers my shyness
looking down this way at the union of mountains and rivers
Floating clouds are flying gowns, spring water glides into a ravine
the sun shines through chilled light on your reclining pose
Often you are uneasy; with the veins of jagged cliffs
colors of boulders, and water charm of reeds
you remind me how to trudge down a long road
how to pass beyond adversity and rejection
So close to you

with my earliest adoration and burning coldness
my loveless heart seemingly without a thought
tumbling swiftly
toward the reflective mirage of the supreme void a thousand feet below—
like a black vulture
cutting through aroused coolness
With each visit
I lift an unfamiliar layer of the earth's garment
The inscriptions on her ancient skin were once familiar
though my spirit wavers because of human turmoil
hesitating now and then between ecstasy and compassion
With each visit I feel
you both familiar and strange, accepting me but complaining
with bright thousand-layered eyes
with the season's breath
shrieking swallows and sparrows, and stream-surfacing shells
So close to you, I look down for
the direction of passionate echoes, call your name
gently as you look up at me, a survivor
bending down like this, like a proud dragon
swooping down to the reflective mirage of a supreme void a thousand
        feet below
searching for your origin
approaching the center of the earth where no one has ever been
with burning flames on a lake of ice—
that was the beginning, when we met
on a spot no longer charted in memory's latitudes and longitudes
then lost each other in the thunder
I have returned after a life of wandering, you lie uneasily
looking up. Yes, suppose this time
we use your perspective as the vantage point, this time
when I, a survivor, bend forward from the edge and look down . . .

1984

# In Imitation of "Poetry of Fields and Garden"

As if in the heart of the city—
in the middle of a vast field, bronze statues
are serious, dutiful scarecrows; light and sparrows
flutter and test the sky. (Don't be afraid, don't be afraid)
We walk up, stop, are about to turn
Distant clouds come from behind the peaks
bells in the temple wait to chime
thunder like wine brewing
tiny fish swimming and growing
In the middle of the field
crops are near harvest and scarecrows
like bronze statues in the city
intimidate our light and our birds
flapping their wings and chirping, quickly landing
then flying back to the power lines of midsummer
they compose a prelude to fall

We purposely leave behind abundant
grain in the harvested field
and take down the scarecrows one by one
We let sparrows flutter from here to there, pick up grain in sunlight
Don't be afraid, come down and eat your fill, then
hurry back to the power lines to repeat your familiar theme:
stock grazing on the riverbank
forty-one sheep should be
enough for you to knit a new coat for me
dozing cattle a little slow-witted
like me

This takes place in the heart of the city
Clever people in pitched battle, statues

the only just witnesses, dropping their powerless hands
We walk on, searching for something
Faraway clouds condense into rain
bells in the temple, drums in the wilderness
thunder and lightning pass through joyfully shouting limbs
fish swarm into the lake of reeds and waterlily pads

1984

## Autumn Song

Most of the stars have returned to their fixed
positions on time, and each holds
a segment of time to control the tides, their ebb and flow;
        witnesses to —
in those darker days and after, our ancestors chose
the earth when most stars had already completed their migration —
emotions in the clanking human world, where people
in an atmosphere that gradually cools
lean on each other, love, complain, doubt
suspect each other's sincerity with the lyricism of songs and tears
then leave the place of parting, offer their views
for the sea to interpret, decorate swift homing paths with reeds
A bird in the cage
a mirror on the face

Most of the stars
most of them have clustered
become flourishing troops in the void of the universe
calculated distance between stars of the third, second
and first class based on revelations of myth and poetry
and arranged themselves to glow according to fixed proportion, and
        people feign
sadness as they walk to the street corner after movies and listen closely
        to the forsaken bell
In broken memories, the prosody of songs and tears
kicks leaves on the road and walks against the wind
when most stars cry out softly at the unusual degree of brightness
shining on our bloated city
like a water-soaked drum

Most of the stars pick up the names they unwittingly lost that day
that day in the pollen-filled human world, they disembodied one by one
faded into the void beyond void until this moment when they pick up
    again
proudly, under the instruction of the heavy barometer
and display poses that fit their names. But
the people all sneak back under the roof and sit there worried
they turn their eyes to goldfish bowls and walnuts and caged birds
to the faces in the mirror, even to an open astronomical map
drooping wisely, when outside in the alley
a truck loaded with rice wine drives slowly by
Cancer is the first to be aware
so it hides a pincer

Yes, most of the stars
have returned to their fixed positions as expected
like pomelos and honeydews stacked on changing temperatures
and fast-dissolving humidity, exuding the smell of rice paddies turned
    over for other crops
covering TV antennas and monitoring them freely
each occupying a commercial break. Eternal patterns
these dark days, on earth we finally reaffirm
that most stars have matured completely
people return from farmland and logging camp, from net fishing at sea
to the city like fruit dropping on a tight, parched drum
All the birds sing outside their cages
faces smile in mirrors

1984

# Song of Yesterday's Snow

Yesterday when it dropped down to mid-mountain, I could feel the
    snow line
(in the dim afternoon) coming near
continuing to drop, flying white over dark green
coniferous treetops, a guidance, desire of the universe
A few surviving leaves, two winter birds perched outside the window blinds
all the chimneys stood still and smokeless
When the snow line finally reached midlevel
people were on their way home from the other side of the mountain
with skis and ice skates on the tops of their cars. So I imagine
randomly, picturing what it was probably like, because
it dropped to the six-hundred foot level yesterday
when I, too, picture it sliding down
the sounds of rivers and sea in my ear, the hesitant
wind, and an intermittent electric saw from the next block

Electric saw? Work unfinished in autumn continues diligently
in the cold weather, like an ancient glutton's teeth
Work unfinished before summer gnaws ferociously at
the fibers of fallen leaves, like the senses
chasing a lock of hair tied with a crimson scarf
A nimble saw cuts across dusks and dawns of the past
lands on the next block, maybe farther and deeper
into a yard, or in water, on the sound waves of a transistor radio
clamoring about the first time the snow line's dropped
to mid-mountain this winter. We have a hunch
it will continue to pick up speed, maybe
before I'm even aware, and glide to the top of
the Lutheran Church on the slope, then fall
silently, finally landing outside our windows, when I too will fall

It falls now. Snow piles on the walls
it has come down to rest at a location close to
sea level. I gather the few hesitant footprints
on the patio must belong to a squirrel or
two, who came and left when we weren't paying attention
All the exits are closed
no car sounds for a ten-mile radius, people stay inside their houses
Luckily there is plenty of food and wine in the basement
They get out of bed, have some soup, sit by the fireplace and listen
to weather forecasts, bathe, go to bed. Snow still falls merrily—
luckily, there are good supplies of birth control pills and vitamin C in
        the cabinet
Snow still falls merrily, lower than the bed sheets
lower than the hills and valleys of the pillows
lower than our shoulders—falling merrily

Falling, snow will probably pile high in dreams
Since yesterday it has occupied our minds with its happy form
in my complete consciousness, and
provides evidence that even if it fills
the comforter's hills and valleys, it is still soft
maintaining a constant temperature like our bodies
so I imagine randomly. When it first touches
the coniferous forest in the distance, I can hear the surging
blood, the breath of love and beauty, and
the nimble electric saw coming intermittently from the next block—
an incomplete autumn sonata
When I enter the region of hills and valleys higher than the snow line
the melody seems to be the expected theme of our new song
slaughtering and destroying the coniferous forest: desire of the universe

1985

# Spring Song

When lingering snow falls from the branches
I see the first cardinal of the year
skipping across the wet patio—
like a prisoner of conscience returning from far away
revealing determination in indifference—
wings glistening with the light of the southern temperate zone
he is a witness to the ultimate universalism
Such a common, believable theory
is mentioned every day, in preschool
classrooms, in laundry women's chitchat, in
the rightists' training class and the leftists' salon
in a soldier's fear and expectation
a mistress's recurrent dream: the omnipresent theory
of the ultimate universalism, he says
is repeated by people in every corner of the earth
at every minute. All in all
spring is here

Now he stops in front of my potted mountain pine
and peeks around. The lingering snow on the roof
melts quickly, pouring its abundance into the flower beds—
"Maybe my heart is vaster than
the universe," I challenge
as I stare at the cardinal's short beak, gentle, inarticulate
his feathers glistening from the caress of a long southern sojourn—
the most reliable light in this awkward season:
"Otherwise, what can you rely on
as you journey?"

"I rely on love," he says
suddenly raising the level of our conversation
Flapping his shiny wings, he skips into the clump of chrysanthemums
that were planted last autumn and survived the bitter winter
"I rely on the power of love, a common
notion, a practice. Love is our guide"
He stands among green leaves and moss-dotted stream rocks
abstract, distant, like a teardrop
quivering in its roundness in the fast-warming air
"Love is the god of the heart . . ." Besides
spring is here

1985

# Synopsis

In Amsterdam
warm morning light shines through windows that open one
at a time, surprise and bashfulness
instantly feigned by people, some quaint curiosity
and hazy looks dispersing in sequence from six floors up
when warm morning light shines through
in Amsterdam. I stand at the head of the glittering bridge
examine your style and complexion from a distance
Familiar desires and resentment drift in the air
warmth and cold nurture a kind of sluggishness
morning sunbeams projected onto the center of the canal
splashing up shrieks at the edge of eternity

It's a memory from the seventeenth century
tumbling in a thousand schools of fish among green algae
mosquitoes hovering over the water. If it were the seventeenth century—
flocks of white birds flying from the Rhine, noisy
as they cross the colonial building by the harbor, the bell tolling six times
a few intellectuals taking a walk on the street, exchanging
ideas about the Enlightenment, discussing Paris, London, India
and Formosa—we can reminisce like this
with an affection that we can't bear to part with and an overdose of
      indifference
at once close and far, trying to cooperate desperately in time's giant river
of regret and happiness, with blood and flesh
with stubborn bones, a pool of hot sweat
with tears that secretly fall when you awake at midnight
and face swaying willow shadows outside the window—we can
      reminisce this way

In Amsterdam

the fact is it's all been proven to be too late

My pride more blurry than Rembrandt's oils

and once cracked, it will continue

to collapse, like a blood-dripping wild duck on the canvas

an extinguished lamp, an overturned basket of beans

In Amsterdam

when the noontime city din has dyed the shade under the trees

the color of motors, we sit on the verandah

looking at the map while we fan hard with a straw hat: windmills

cattle ranches, tulip farms, yacht docks

Our brows and lips exhume the smell of fat and knowledge

as we seriously discuss, debate, compromise

In the square of the train station, flocks of greedy pigeons flutter

In front of the colonial building the statue of the old king in a

       military outfit

looks grand with his presumptuous sword. I can't help snickering

and consequently forcing all the impatience into a smile:

"Well, it's okay

if you like it this way"—although all this

has long since been proven to be too late


1985

# A Test of Autumn

I hear garden shears snapping outside my window—
the sharp sound knocks in the wind with pleasure
The morning sun sprinkles high and low over grass and trees
I lift my head, distracted from my cup, and look outside
searching. The shadows on the wall are the color of oolong tea
the shears cavalierly fly through low hedges and small trees
A gentle, benevolent slaughter goes on
and on. I lean out the window; the sound
suddenly gets louder, fills the neighborhood
but there's no trace of the gardener
The beech is heavy with crimson nuts
the leaves on the old maple seem ready to fall
the arbor of ripe grapes behind the mossy path
beneath the pine tree two bundles of twigs
with most of the chrysanthemums in bud
I walk into the yard, searching; there's no trace of the gardener
inside or outside the walls, only the sparkling morning breeze brushing by,
    cool as the cup of tea
He plies these clacking shears. It's him
He's the god of the seasons, testing me with the same sharpness and
    patience

1985

# Frost at Midnight

'Tis calm, indeed, so calm, that it disturbs
And vexes meditation with its strange
And extreme silentness.

Samuel Taylor Coleridge


Like pushing aside layers of reed stalks, at summer's end
when the aroma of firewood through chimneys wafts gently in the air
comes to me creeping low, on a soft breeze—a calling
unfolds delicately, yet seems just around my eyelids—
when the color duckweed, swaying in clumps, stirs up bits of memory
when the long-tailed dragonfly flies toward me, hesitant
and trembling, it hovers above the twilight-dyed ripples
and tries to land on a thorny water plant
scattering powdery pistils, making dusk return to the swiftly
changing moment when I push aside layers and layers of reed stalks
like pushing aside layers and layers of reed stalks at the end of that
    faraway summer

So I see, like the last ashes in an incense burner
in front of the already dim altar that insists on shouting
in silence, trying hard to elevate the instant to an eternal memory
in my faint unease like transparent moth wings flapping
outside the window, sound of dried, broad leaves like hearts, blowing
    about one by one
circling in the wind before falling at random into the cool shade of
    the empty courtyard
I see an expanse of light on the startled pond at summer's end
lingering at ease, softly chanting a long, ancient tune, intending to
turn fate into luck when frogs croak at intervals in the lonely hour
when crickets besiege childhood wilderness, when I push aside layers
    and layers of reed
stalks to find time slowly transcending summer's end

# Part Four
### 1986–1991

## Fish Festival

We have come to the appointed spot
snow on the mountains, tulips not yet in bud
To the east, most passes are closed
but the ferryboat in the west sails the tumbling waves as usual
On a day when the sun
brightens the riverbanks and piers
folks from the suburbs or farther
come by different routes to gather here
Some are just getting started, but we
have already arrived

Before noon a breeze skims the river
The sea is probably on the other side of the hill
I smell salt
and a stagnant rustiness in the air
It's early, we got the best spot; from here I can see
the streets in the village have been swept clean
a few flagpoles stand at the intersections, just as before
As before, seagulls spread their wings and dip low
or they perch on the balcony rail while we imagine
that from a certain direction
schools of silver-finned smelt — the most punctual travelers —
are swimming downstream to the appointed spot

We arrived a little early
and forgot to bring the right fishing equipment
On this eve before the festival, we imagine how numerous
gleaming fish in the river — like silent, distant stars
reflecting each other and taking turns twinkling in the Milky Way —
light up each other's tails as they float in the familiar
direction, between determination and idleness

like a prolonged folk song
repeating the same melody over and over
They are the most punctual travelers
In a big, icy river
they drink water, flutter their fins, swing their tails
following too closely, bump into one another
With half-open eyes, they glide downstream
between pride and shyness
for we have arrived at the appointed spot
while starlike silver-finned fishes are hurrying along
toward the mouth of the same river. Suddenly

a seagull's shrill cry cuts across the sandy beach
Startled, we look at each other, then lower our heads
only to find in the sparkling water—
there they are, they have arrived

1986

# I Came from the Sea

But they, like fantasies from a previous life
When I wander through the countryside and its roaring spring surf
a fragmented tune fills the wild and sways with the wind
two, three baskets sit aslant on the ridge of the field
Then, unexpectedly, you and I meet by the corner of the old
city wall; your uncertain look spreads toward the water
I sense the clash of cartwheels and banners
In the distance, on roads I have yet to travel
many things will happen as they must
Surf surges behind us, and farther away, an island
a noisy pier, marketplace, temple
still farther, the sea

I came from the sea

1986

# Lamp

When I see pine needles fill the courtyard after rain
morning light flickers by the stone wall, on the lawn
duckweed floating in the pond has turned from fresh green to sallow
and gaunt eyes and brows quietly
quietly teach love and hate . . . when I see
forget, then suddenly remember
the courtyard filled with pine needles after rain
floating duckweed in the pond in flickering morning light
gaunt love and hate, I imagine a gusty wind from last night
coming from the faraway sea, in the dark
causing pine needles to dance wildly in the sky . . . like teary eyes
The universe cries freely in an obscure moment
blinks its confused eyes in an instant of human neglect
When the gusty wind came last night, followed by a shower
beating on the sleepy courtyard, I seemed to
be aware—but in fact was bewildered—
that dormant in a corner of the forest of my consciousness
I timidly search my mind: Was it that
lonely, obscure moment when a gusty wind followed by a drizzle
invaded the abyss where I took shelter? Gnawed inwardly, did I
recall the celestial revelation between the real and the illusive
as if relating the ebb and flow of tides, the growth and
decline of time, ridges and capes as dimensions of life?
So I hear the frequency of the tree rings' revolution
see the tracks of the constellations' movements
leaving a few echoes and scars. Then I, too
fall asleep and wake up on the dreamless edge
and drowsily patrol at the back of my shady consciousness
At the moment the universe weeps in an obscure place
and speaks of loneliness, pine needles filling the sky

dance wildly. Only I guard it
with a lamp flickering in my heart
only I guard it
with a lamp in my heart

1986

# In Fact

Loud as the water flowing over my head
In a corner of deep virginal forest
I wait for someone to come
someone in a blouse like dazzling spring sun
her round arms bare like reborn
lilies swaying in the breeze
of my memory and oblivion

So I hope, waiting
among dense bushes, adding fuel to my limbs
my thought, a blast furnace, temperature steadily rising
With my head on a granite boulder, I listen to water flowing
night and day, the howl of growing grass
the cries of multiplying insects. In fact
nothing has happened

1987

# Wind Chime

Rain stopped, wind tight, sparse sunlight
slants southeast. I hear
a delicate sound shuttling around the house's corners
imagine it to be a missed intention from the past
turning into seasonal clouds and mist after
a certain indifference, returning
awakening with a start
I imagine it is memory
memory's windchime
loudly shaking an autumn afternoon
that once was ours. When sunlight tests
the warmth of the water tank, throws a rippling
reflection on the ceiling
and stares at a clamorous, splashing bed
I look, silently count the wave-surging
colors as they change directly above me
like auras, clouds, stars
rising and falling in order
like rhythm

I hear
the chime tumble over
the harvested melon patch
run into the wall, then bounce through a half-open window
No longer indecisive, it leaps up to my bed and leans against
someone's flushing cheek. Hair
wandering, eyes hazy—
at this moment, music fills
excited blood vessels, ten thousand tributaries
born in dream's ancient pool, spreading
up and down and into another ten thousand tributaries

born in dream's ancient pool—
there they meet and converge
in an overwhelming flood

I imagine it is memory
memory's loud windchime drifting across
an autumn afternoon
that once was ours

1987

# Lama Reincarnated

*A Tibetan lama died in San Francisco; some years later*
*they realized that he'd been reincarnated in Spain.*

They looked for me everywhere, starting in Kashmir
going southeast along the Ganges
through wilderness and villages, under scorching sun, in rainstorms
past river gorges and mountain bends

Then they split into two groups:
one crossed the Irrawaddy River, pushing anxiously
eastward, across the Salween and Mekong
searched every pagoda and temple

The other group crossed the Indian subcontinent
turned to war-ravaged Afghanistan
endured hunger, fatigue, and error
before they entered ancient Galilee

When they entered Galilee with their alms bowls
on the way to visit the birthplace of Jesus
suddenly an explosion near the stone bridge—
a bomb set off by terrorist revenge

Total mystification; gore
and violence are nowhere to be found
in their scriptures. They were unaware
the eastward group had just arrived in Korea

Pigeons fluttered through the teargassed air. Cornered by
riot police, a young student
poured gasoline on himself and struck a match
With a loud cry, he leaped back, trailing smoke and angry flames in
    his wake

The monks turned out en masse, speaking one by one
in the square, while the other group left Galilee
along the magi trail
but in that frosty night they couldn't find the star

They sat deferentially on the bus, hardly talking to each other
Traveling day and night, they reached the seaside, boarded a ship
and arrived on shore, following another myth. Europe
with fig trees in every direction, but where could they find me?

At night they meditated by themselves. Outside the tavern
the nihilist Balkan Peninsula was in an uproar
wine flowed like fresh blood. They held a meeting
and decided first to go north to try the frigid zone.

They didn't know the other group
had already changed planes in Tokyo
and crossed the Pacific to North America, entering
a Mexico that seemed to hold possibility

They changed into their light yellow cloaks
hired a donkey cart, and visited many small towns
Everywhere people played the guitar
as they sang over and over again: "Andalusia . . ."

The sea breeze fluttered against their searching eyes. They traveled
across many long and narrow countries this way
Sometimes helicopters appeared in the sky
chop, chop, chopping into pieces that Andalusia

It was fortunate the other group
decided to turn around when they got to the Baltic Sea
though they couldn't help getting lost in the Black Forest
When spring came, they at last straggled into Morocco on foot

They sat on the ground, depressed, not knowing where their next stop
should be. To the east lay Italy (amen!)
to the west lay Spain (amen!). Church bells were
ringing everywhere: Where could they find me?

Africa? Perhaps their reincarnated guru
would appear in the Congo: a young lama of the Black Sect of Tantric
    Buddhism
They got up, dusted themselves off, and decided on the spot
to board a ship and sail straight to Gibraltar

That day they walked more than a hundred kilometers
thinking about the Congo all the while. They heard
donkey hooves clattering beyond the horizon
loving guitar melodies kept them company

Someone was singing at ease under a fig tree:
"Andalusia . . ." The song
arched across the parched plains. "Come with me
come with me to Andalusia"

They left the forked road. Lilies
bloomed on the golden hills
sparrows were flitting past, muskrats scampered
in the dry fields. I called softly to the wind:

"I am in Granada
Bring me the insignia from my previous life:
my crown of gold, staff, rosary, and robes and cloaks
Bring them to Granada, Andalusia"

By now the other group had traveled around
the tip of Chile. They, too, heard my whisper:
"I am in Granada." They looked left and right at the ocean:
"Granada? Ah — Andalusia"

Come, come, come to Andalusia
come find me, find me in faraway Granada
Let us sing and praise eternal Granada
a golden flower blooming in Andalusia

Come, come, come to Andalusia
come find me, find me in faraway Granada
Let us sing and praise eternal Granada
let us sing a new song about old Andalusia

1987

# Facing the Fog with Ming-ming
## on December Seventeenth

The fog gradually recedes, leaving water marks
A place cold and faraway, beyond imagination — maybe
a gorge with new-fallen snow — that's
the place where it returns in silence

That must be it
A young beast's gentle call from the other shore
leaves light, shy footprints for next year's
new sunshine to sort out

Are these traces of the fog's flight? Lost on an ice-cold path
it once flew indecisively over our eaves
played on the windchime, and looked doubtfully
at seven nodding purple bamboo

It turns and leaves
but its disgruntled eyes are the pale light that shines above
as we keep watch in a small house on the slope
and fog gradually recedes, leaving water marks

1988

# Three Etudes: The Snake

1.

Someone asked something and
before I could answer, hid in the murmuring woods
I looked around
the greenness in my heart faded in the dappled light:
heaven and earth a zebra

So I stood quietly, thinking:
"His doubt was inevitable, even if
forbidden." Then from a high treetop
a leaf fell gently in E-flat minor
shaped like lips slightly open, swaying elegantly
fluttering, with delicate trills, through a bright halo into a dazzling pose
lighting aslant a spider web. Another
mottled ray swept across one corner of the lips, illuminating them
an instant. He asked about my train of thought. Yet
he is rooted in a frigid, northern island in this stately forest
a melancholy dissident in the
cool shady depths of this forest
inclined to solitary living

His palette—
flying yellow and swift green, like the satin ribbons billowing behind a
        T'ang terra-cotta figurine
he's a sash loosened from a woman's body after armor-clad midnight
when she awakes at the beginning of that shadowy year that follows
        the dragon
Eyes gleaming with the cold light of a firefly, he examines his slender form
and is deeply shocked: "Beauty comes from ancient time
it's a mystical experience, fear-inspiring
with a touch of evil—but that's a misunderstanding"

Actually, except for shyness he has no flaws
he's not even unsociable

though inclined to solitary living. That day
he swam to me swiftly in the grass, swooshing like a waterfall
assumed a soaring-swooping posture, and congealed
into a historical monument
He seemed to be asking about my troubles. While I hesitated
a leaf fell *allegretto sforzando*
He turned and retreated into
the depths of the forest — this melancholy
dissident

2.

She may have a heart (the reeds shake their heads and look
equivocal). If she did, it would be cold anyway
I ran in the direction in which she vanished, and guessed about this
Under the cliff, the vines, the spring
the noonday sun intermittently shone on piles of pebbles
she sat cross-legged, furious and dejected

silently blaming herself in a place no one knew
her ice-cold body doubled over, then doubled again
Still she could not stir a long dead passion; instead
she knew that where head joins body, where reason and emotion
clash, there is a kind of trembling
The welcome spring drizzle drifts by, warm as undried tears from a
    former life

She must have a heart, must have had one
once, tightly wrapped inside her brilliantly colorful gown, beating
awaiting transmigrations and inevitable doom in some foreseeable age
dissolving somewhere to the left of the gallbladder
And so she sat cross-legged on the pebbles, dejected and blaming
    herself. Why?
The reeds shake their heads and look equivocal

3.
So I speculated, sitting in boredom
on a north-inclining cliff on this planet, listening to the waves pound jumbled
    rocks
I imagined snakes to be androgynous
like angels. Lifting my head, I saw the clouds tumbling above:
some were like gaily laughing faces, others like tightly knit brows
I thought the androgynous snake
must be the progeny of a winged creature
especially since they can be viviparous and lay eggs

Before the cool of autumn, the snakes completed their mating
in some dew-soaked wilderness
The male slithered away from the spot, never to return—
like grass decomposing on the ground, turning into mud, and then
    into fireflies—
leaving the female alone, bewildered and uneasy, unsure
whether to lay eggs this time or produce live young
Falling into a deep reverie, she tried to decide
then remembered:
How many painless moltings have I been through?
In the hollow of an old tree, in a pile of dead leaves, in a barn or a
    deserted kiln
surrounded by chirping birds
I have tried on my new gown in the soft spring breeze:
"Beauty is continuous creation, based on archetypes
of something not deviating from the principle behind ancestral
    patterns and colors"
Yet beauty knows no gender in their world, the world of
a species, once winged, that has
evolved into crawling reptiles

Even so
the brooding snake could not help feeling resentful
when the setting sun retreated from the surface of the water, leaving

concentric ripples undulating in the fast-darkening bay
and separated cosmic secrets with the seven colors of the rainbow
in an artful and dazzling moment
Like angels, not bound by tradition or discipline or norms
invisible, indomitable, sounding clarions or caroling
having earned our respect and given us joy with their androgynous bodies
it realized that his disappearance
rendered her transformations meaningless. All this
I came to understand before I fell asleep:
heaven and earth were like a molted skin

1988

## Dance: A Solo

Her soul damned by God, a dancer in black
flies across memory
through its frosty woods
Her chin held high, parallel to the water
her eyes reach beyond human sights
and sounds. Smiles and teardrops miss her ears
and enter the ganglion
to be classified
stored
forgotten

Only her pupils search
for the loftily floating, luminous objects in the sky
She aims at some and ignites them
one by one
strikes them down
then swiftly hits the others
with empty choreography past
memory's moist beach
leaving a track of light, lonely footprints. "Come to me," God says
"Come to me so I can speak to you"

Her hands sway like the fins of fish
When the ocean's temperature changes abruptly, she
relaxes her hands, gestures, lowers her speed
Suddenly she darts, turns, swims with her short tail
swings quietly like coral in primeval wilderness
her limbs rosy
her joints destroyed by pure love
Her limbs have always been
her

best
language

Neither shy nor
shrewd, she arches her back and drops her head
till she nears a spot in the wild clover field
Through moistened lashes she fixes her gaze
on a bright-colored insect perching between leaves and petals
Startled, she rises and darts across my unintended
shadow, my haphazardly cast shadow
That year
in the waterlily pond (when moonlight
filled the meadow and overflowed into the pond)
my shadow rocked in the water and lost its spirit
Casually she picked it up, flew over fireflies
ice skates, knitting needles, daffodils
a dancer in black—
"Come to me," God says
"so I can speak to you"

1989

# Dance: A Duo

Walking east-northeast
you disappear into the woods
But you still quiver and gleam in
my eyes, gestures, footfalls
my tangible existence
Can I see you or not? I can
only feel you, bathed in sunlight
gently tiptoeing
gliding
where mushrooms grow

The morning fog behind you
has begun to dissipate; tree branches
mimic your splayed fingers —
moving left and right like a Thai dancer, enhanced by shoulder movement
When a giant river cuts through the plateau where fire and water meet
I hear rock formations cry for release beneath the black soil
You lower your head, twirl swiftly between waking and sleep
Sunlight splashes like the cogs of a wheel
thunder and lightning wrap tightly around you

All is complete with my
approval; my vision beyond time and space
guides all your steps and gestures
You hear a brook in the distance
alert and ready, you rise
walk forward, following my eyes
stop at the spot I specify. You turn
and fall like a skiff
gliding from the brook into a placid lake
toward clumps of lotuses

1990

# Song: Departing

Departing. A rain shower in my heart
two or three yellow flowers tremble in my senses
The wind, an Impressionist pioneer, flies
gently past the long bridge over the river, main streets and alleys
to meet me where willows tangle with streetlights

A theme forgotten but now remembered
once melted into an octave fence
like the small beast of sunlight on a chilly autumn night
disappearing under your gaze. Startled, you awake
and stand alone, knowing it has returned in silence

Returned? I let myself be struck, again and again
by pale thunder hidden in long ago city sounds
certain that its hand aims straight at deep sorrow, stunned
as if I slowly knelt in the bright light coming
through window blinds and the clock's sallow ticking

Tomatoes in bloom, the sky over the small garden the same
juicy and sweet with a hint of sour, as if
the beginning of the universe
manifest between real and false stars, is just now
taking shape beyond the clouds before my arrival

What a lonely time that must be!
Even if beautiful as a strange land, a land without me!
On both sides of the railroad tracks, hazy wild grass, grasshoppers —
looking from the upstairs window, I see spring flowers
in yellow and white, dancing butterflies

Only I have come late. Maybe
I'm always bewildered like an autumn night
I listen to a giant palm shed a tremendous frond —

there must be a message in this, about
flourish and decay, time and parting

That's the wind's perennial game
hanging up the sunset when you're lost in thought
Shuttling across a pear farm and an automobile factory
he spies on you like a poet of the sentimentalist school:
under a silent lamp, quiet before tea, a single pure chrysanthemum

A touch of self-pity, even liking to discuss it
maybe like the pensive narcissus musing
on its own invisible blood and body—
I always know and have no need to
ask, otherwise no one in the world
could understand the rhythm of my language

Depart, depart. I look for this old title in
ancient Music Bureau poetry in a book trunk. It's never forgotten
but it exists not in a book trunk, only in my heart
The wind is a postmodernist who has lost his identity
barging into my room, he finds me writing swiftly as a daemonic child

1989

# In Front of a Squadron of Tanks

In front of a squadron of tanks, someone said
you stood firm and blocked their way
while the tracks clanked and twitched. Then I said
heaven and earth hold their breaths, the world is watching you

So I said. In my car on the way home
I listened to the anchorman read a telegram from Beijing
under his breath: "A man in a white shirt . . ."
The clamoring sea finally quiets down

In the square that has witnessed countless struggles and
killings, a dazzling ray of light shines from ancient times
your ancestors' eyes shining on the armor
a small banner, and your quiet dark hair

The air is filled with rifts from swishing
arrow and wounding lance. Yesterday and today
flee helter-skelter, groaning and screaming
A creased, yellowed book of history

broken spears long buried under the earth
glory and shame go their separate ways
A glaring squadron of tanks marches on, and
at the command of gods and ghosts it brakes with a screech, for you

Then the engines restart
steel balls clash with fuel, raising
a bloodthirsty howl in the dusty wind
monumental columns throwing shadows to the left

You stand firm, the news anchorman says
Now the east side of the city is quiet, but in the west
sporadic explosions can be heard
A mighty tank squadron in panic

like a troop of ants running into
a waterdrop, crystal clear, cold to the bone
You are an ancestor's tear falling into the flame
a scalding teardrop blocking their way

Your youthful forehead shines bright
facing the cannon just shifted to shooting range
The track belts change direction with a roar. You take one step forward
and start giving a speech in front of them

In the distance, crows sit quietly on the city wall
moss and grass wither and fall from the tower
a bell slowly tolls to the mountains, steadily, lovingly, the sea
surges toward dazzling coastal islets

In the distance, reed catkins sway and quiver by the ferry
outcroppings sleep and dream in a primitive forest
newborn colts gallop across the prairie
raising their heads and at the same time listening

In the distance travelers sit one by one, watching
the scampering wind and clouds. The red sun over a vast lake
hesitates to choose a direction to turn
A flute wafts across a faraway

orchard where sprinklers suddenly stop
unripe cherries languish in the mist
Workers sit and read newspapers quietly; they hear that in China
someone with dark hair and a white shirt refuses to budge

In the distance cogs inextricably tangle with chains
whistles turn hoarse, people in cars step on their brakes
pull to the shoulder of the freeway, and adjust
the dial—a Chinese man is going to give a speech

On the way home I hear the clamoring
sea, the twitching and clanking of tracks
And yes, before a squadron of tanks, someone says
you stand firm, blocking their way

Heaven and earth hold their breath, the whole world is watching you
Then I say: crystal clear and bitterly cold
you are your ancestor's tear, scorched red and burning hot with flame —
a tear that drops in choked compassion

1989

You'll Come Back Alive
*An Elegy for Those Who Died*
*in the June 4, 1989, Massacre*

Like reeds shivering in the autumn wind, sparkling water
reflecting the broken shadows of flowers and leaves, like reeds . . .
Strange, each time I think of them
standing or lying down, in the square soaked with tears and bloody sweat
surrounded by heavy armament—even though
it's all in the past, the past
I still shiver, like reeds in an autumn wind
and my heart sinks slowly to the bottom of a cold dark stream

I see Time bending over me
picking me up. Like a mother, she tenderly
rearranges broken body and will, washes away
tears and bloody sweat—forlorn traces of my memory—
smoothes my hair, and buttons my shirt
No more shouting and crying for
the shouts and cries in the scorching sun, I thought. But no
my limbs turn cold each time I think of . . .

Someone says their feet went astray
their slogans transient and empty as bubbles
their colorful banners undisciplined, inconsistent
even contradicting each other, illogical and ineffectual
As to the fist? I see a fist relaxing
It was raised as a symbol—from the long lost
sixties of morning coffee
tobacco in the afternoon, and midnight rage and regret
We understand the symbol, yet surely it was their feet
in those old days that went astray

White cloth bands around their heads, a manifesto
in vermilion and black pointing to the northern sky
Chinese characters—in simplified form or complex—but far more
    complex than
the words were their tortured anxiety
and repressed will. Their spirit was blowing
blowing, with resolve, toward a shoreless dreamland
beard-studded chins, nearsighted and astigmatic
they looked up at the memorial statues of people's heroes
Braids ending in ribbons, the lost are
lost, the dead will never come back

"I panicked and clutched the current
The rapids carried me far far away
and tossed me on the rocky shore . . ."
Tossing him into fiery twilight
face down, right shoulder slightly higher than left
That incident took place some time ago, but
strange, each time I think of him
I still feel a tightness in my chest

"Actually, I didn't really die"
he humored me: "I walked through
a vast ruin where wild grass
mixed with sprouting wheat . . ." Robins hop
Up and down on the pulley of a dried-up well, crows squawk
I don't know if you're gone. I walked with you
through the endless ruin. Even if you are dead
I know you'll come back alive

1989

# The Day after Easter

The day after Easter
I miss him and his atheism badly
Pigeons cross the sky outside my window
downstairs, shouts, each louder than the one before:
it's the minister's only daughter pulling a crowd together
to march to the square
The shy lily on my desk—
like swans, pumpkin, and the king's deer
in legends—
is heartbreaking. Last night
when I walked to the mouth of the alley with it, the Bible study group
was still singing. The lights and music were equally faithful and brave
proclaiming how long ago, in an obscure moment
the Son of Man came to life again and ascended to heaven
This is the day after Easter
yet how desperately
I miss
his atheism
and him

1990

## Village Sonnets

1. On the Other Side
I wonder how things are on the other side
Here, a wind is pecking at the tapestry woven with the rays
of autumn sun. Transparent traces instruct me
but as I look above and below, I hear
a faint and tender echo
through the chords of my memory—
a saxophone in the courtyard

It's a lyrical tale
before the modern age
Born in the cool of a shady sidestreet
its curious notes bounced off stone walls
In search of sunlight, they rose higher
than flowers in window boxes
higher than bells, dove cages, and beehives

2. Here in the Rain
Here in the rain I see the color of her dress
is like the color of the one she wore in a previous life, wet
as she emerged from the fig grove
her lips and hair wet
her arms cool to the touch. A faraway village—
we occupied it with equal shares of joy and
melancholy. In the early morning
we walked on a narrow road lined with olive trees
At noon, unexpectedly warm
we sat in a bistro listening
to young singers talk about zodiac signs
and blood types. In the afternoon we just waited
till earth and sky turned dark. And here
"If it is predestined, I am afraid"

3. I Lie Back in the Rocking Chair
So am I
As I lie back in the rocking chair, I am
a little tired. I glance at
the fruit that will soon ripen in the autumn sun
and I feel complete. Then, as in the past
I let my limbs float above consciousness, drained
but senses keen and groping
toward a single string—
we occupy it
with equal shares of joy and melancholy
we speak about past and future . . .
Present? Earth and sky suddenly turn dark
animals stampede like our apprehensions
toward the haze
A saxophone plays in the courtyard

1990

# In Lieu of a Letter

Then the sky and earth begin to expand
touching reefs, islets
in the roll and tumble of gentle waves
in opaque, profound
adulation: the heart is the reflection of the universe
We look for hidden teachings, send the scout
on a detour, let love and hate follow against the current
There's a gentle rise in distant hills
a seagull
flaps its wings unhurriedly, then swoops down
then another seagull mimics it with determination

This is entirely possible, attainable—
now as water vapor rises
and clings to our bodies
sunlight shimmers before us to the left
knocking against two pairs of dazed eyes
like the moment our palms touch, the moment
tears rest on cheeks, wind blows across
a railing, blood surges into the heart
rain moistens the loquat blooming near the balcony

In silence I repeatedly arrange
one or two sentences. But
giving up without a word is finally most beautiful
even though I'd still like to speak
Then I think, if we just sit here like this
on an idle afternoon
facing the intermingling sea and sky
cries of waterfowl
coming from the pier now and then . . .

You blink your eyes, lean forward to search
but the birds are already
gone

And you are most beautiful, leaning against
a warm chair
peaceful, trusting, engrossed
with no trace of calculation. Only when your will
in a complete fairytale
gallops side by side with passion across hills and rivers
through wind and rain, sunshine, moonlight
through feasts and adversities, are you most beautiful—
in a large illustrated book
the banner and armor of a knightly vanguard
or in a tryst behind drawn curtains
when two hold the longest gaze
without sentimentality

1991

# For No Reason

Sitting among dry cicada husks
you start worrying
for no reason
Past, present, future . . .
the future?
Hair lightens with each washing
skin translucent from love
you're behind in your piano practice
Suddenly you realize the tea's getting cold
a moment
of bewilderment
In the yard
chrysanthemums seem smaller. You close your eyes
not wanting to look at them but recall your childhood
of surprising crabapple red, peacock
blue, perilla purple, peony yellow . . .
the sound of scissors cutting and wrists
bumping on wooden bolts of fabric
Then you think: When I am old
will I be able to unfold as easily
as satin brocade on a slick surface
to unfold, to spread out, with such dazzle?

1991

## Spring Moon: An Impromptu

Maybe you are the late moon
of this moment, sound
between fresh green trees
speaking, almost perfectly, of the hushed affairs of your heart—
I understand the befores and afters

So deep, so attached, like a zither
fading out of our illuminated world
leaving behind your shiny clean hair, the cool palms of your hands
brilliant, peaceful, telling me
stories of sunny and cloudy days

I listen well, am
moved. Maybe it is at a moment like this
when the late spring moon slowly rises, I realize
I can no longer walk easy with hands behind my back
All I see, floating clouds surging like ocean waves
like the scent of flowers in our breath-stopping world

What you have and have not said, I understand it all
Now I bend forward to look at
the dancing tree shadows on the lawn, or
do nothing at all. My heart full
standing straight, I can admit all my worries

1991

# Fable Number 1: Stone Tiger

Once we were voracious and faint-hearted
like newborn stone tiger cubs
listening in the moonlight
Is that a breeze brushing over the pine grove?
In the prairie beyond, are there bears
their claws clacking along the riverbank?
A night owl mumbles above our heads
below
a snake blinks
as it glides across
rotten leaves
and toadstools and eyes a lizard
Dew drips from the leaves
Once we silently observed
the sound of changing earth and sky, their hues
stand still like newborn stone tigers
watching moonlight tiptoe in the pine grove
through unruly branches
and pounce on the prairie
Standing still
we stare at the grove and
the brilliant darkness outside
our four paws glued to the earth
insisting on a pose
the dignity of a rare species
voracious and faint-hearted
We listen
to the sound of fawns twitching their ears
and squirrels wiggling their tails
The land declines sharply beyond the prairie

In the middle of a ravine
two orange-yellow tents
a campfire
some tunes
and the broken notes of a guitar . . .
Let dewdrops fall
over our necks
shoulders and backs, like once voracious
and faint-hearted stone tigers


1991

# Fable Number 2: Yellow Sparrow

He comes back from the millet field
and relates a shocking incident to me—
his long, dabbled hair unbound, his colored robe
in disarray from tumult, his wrinkled face
tracing dynastic changes
in his left hand a banner held upside down—
no entwined dragons nor phoenix bells
only a faded embroidery of tortoise and bat—
in his right hand, a sword
dustless and bright
He comes back
from the millet field, from the ancient past—
a swordsman in rags
secretly moving through darkness and light
with the memory of an old tale
about a yellow sparrow
caught upside down in a windy net

He'd once been
a buoyant youth from our human world
smartly dressed
equipped with bow and arrows and long sword
dashing on his stallion past a murmuring stream in summer heat
and—before he was aware—into a desolate millet field
on a windy day . . .

It was in the ancient past
he saw the vengeful yellow sparrow
struggling in a net
The wind sighed in tall trees, the ocean
churned in the distant future

He got off his horse and cut the net loose with his sword
The yellow sparrow catapulted into the vacant sky
sending tremors through his heart and soul. Instantly
his hair turned gray
his blood paled, his robe was torn
to pieces, his bow lost
arrows scattered, the color of the banner changed
Only the sword in his right hand, a sword
dustless and bright

He comes back from the millet field
and relates a shocking incident to me


1991

# Fable Number 3: Salmon

When April begins to brighten
the Stillaguamish basin
sunshine swims upstream from the sea's wounded mouth
and crouches, ready to invade the inland
Winding bays and meandering coves
thaw one by one, giving life to
tender green reeds
When reeds sway gently, charming
like fast-growing hair—
the kind that belongs to women in love—
we wait by the edge of
the warm ocean current, testing
the rapid surge of clear water
cool, limpid, and familiar
as if all enticing charms
are melting in the onrushing
Stillaguamish. When we
linger and play, the April sun
brightens my healthy gills, our healthy gills
With a flap of the tail, I turn and point at
the land, toward Stillaguamish

I know, earlier than me
the April sun has already patrolled the Stillaguamish's life and death
When the river excites my gills
I shiver and adjust body temperature
I turn, swim, and dart
swallow stray shrimps and tiny fish to my heart's content
glide among the sprouting reeds
and gnaw on the hair
that belongs to women in love

At Stillaguamish
the narrow gate of life and death opens and shuts
Infinite time, mysterious
origin affirms my vision, foreseeing
across eons of wilderness and the burning dust of
past, present, and future
autumn mountains overgrown in the embrace of
red leaves and the first snow sending chill down the highest peak
when I, on a wounded voyage, face
the most treacherous whirlpool of my life
in the upper stream of Stillaguamish

1991

# Notes to the Poems

"Prophecy":.The Five Dynasties refers to the five short-lived dynasties in the tenth century, following the demise of the glorious T'ang Dynasty (618–907).

"A Sequel to Han Yü's 'Mountain Rocks,' a Seven-Character Poem in the Old Style": Han Yü (768–824) was a statesman, Confucian scholar, and poet of the T'ang Dynasty. In contrast to "recent-style poetry" in Chinese literary tradition, which had matured by the seventh century, the earlier, "old-style" poetry is less bound by rigid prosody and other formal constraints. Li Po (701–62) and Tu Fu (712–70) are hailed by both scholars and general readers as the greatest Chinese poets. While each shows originality and craftsmanship in his work, Li displays Taoist influence, with its emphasis on spiritual freedom and transcendence, and Tu is more Confucian, with a strong sense of social and moral responsibility. Ssu-ma Hsiang-ju (179–117 B.C.E.) is a poet of the Han Dynasty and famous for his elegant rhyme-prose. According to legend, he seduced his wife-to-be with his lute playing.

"Chi-tzu of Yen-ling Hangs Up His Sword": Chi-tzu (576–485 B.C.E.) was a scholar and diplomat during the Spring and Autumn Period (722–481 B.C.E.), the decline of the majestic Chou Dynasty (1111–256 B.C.E.). The Songs refers to The Book of Songs, the first anthology of Chinese poetry from the eleventh to the sixth century B.C.E.; it was edited by Confucius and has been considered a canonical text since it was written. Ch'i and Lu were feudal states in the Spring and Autumn Period. Lu was Confucius' home state.

"The Master" refers to Confucius (551–479 B.C.E.). Both Tzu-lu and Tzu-hsia were Confucius' disciples.

"Geometry: Goddess": The goddess in the title is Ts'ao Chih's goddess (197–226 A.D.) "Rhyme-prose on the Goddess of the Lo River." Lines 17 and 43–45 are quoted from Ch'ü Yuan's (343?–278? B.C.E.) poems "Goddess of the Hsiang River" and "Lady of the Hsiang River," respectively.

"Zeelandia": Taiwan was a Dutch colony in the seventeenth century; Zeelandia was the Dutch name for T'ai-nan, an old city in the south. When the Portuguese came in the sixteenth century, they called Taiwan Isla Formosa (Beautiful Island).

# Index to Titles